The Best
American
Short Plays

2001–2002

The Best American Short Plays

2001–2002

edited with an introduction
by Glenn Young

APPLAUSE THEATRE & CINEMA BOOKS
An Imprint of Hal Leonard Corporation
New York

The Best American Short Plays 2001–2002
Edited with an introduction by Glenn Young

Copyright © 2007 by Applause Theatre & Cinema Books (an imprint of Hal Leonard Corporation)

Published in 2007 by
Applause Theatre & Cinema Books (an imprint of Hal Leonard Corporation)
19 West 21st Street, New York, NY 10010

Printed in the United States of America
Book interior by Pearl Chang

ISBN-13: 978-1-55783-704-2 **ISBN-10**:1-55783-704-X [cloth]
ISBN-13: 978-1-55783-705-9 **ISBN-10**:1-55783-705-8 [paper]
ISSN: 0067-6284

www.applausepub.com

For Peter Alkalay:
ally, friend & collaborator
on many of life's short dramas

contents

introduction
by Glenn Young

David Ives

David Ives ushers us into the musty catacombs of an old Chicago Catholic church where Edna and Flo are celebrating the last rites of a dying way of life. During their elaborate preparations for a funeral breakfast, epiphanies of powdered sugar and ground walnuts flash before us. "Sprinkle, sprinkle, sprinkle, grind, grind, grind" is the sound of incense from the lower depths where the icons of Jesus and the saints have been replaced with nut clusters, "krooshcheeki," and other brands of angel food. It's quite a while before we learn it's Edna and Flo's generous and thoughtful friend Mary who has died, she who was named for the ultimate saint, and for whom the priest scrambled to locate anyone to prepare the burial breakfast. The ingredients are alien to a traditional American palate, and it is through these rare spices and tastes and smells that the writer awakens our appetite for another life, then makes us sad to relinquish it when all is in readiness.

Oh yes, there are signs of degeneration everywhere in **LIVES OF THE SAINTS**. The miracles featured here are the patent medicines sold on late-night TV. And yet there is a measure of grace in Mr. Ives' play. Flo and Edna intone a vibrant and mysterious strain of Pig Latin that would leave a department of Notre Dame linguists scratching their monkish bald spots. Kabuki-like technicians mediate the drama between the '50s and the postmodern void. Ives slows us down, turns us into a collective Margaret Mead, listening to the meaning behind these atavistic phonemes and sounds, of ancient mutterings, of great aunts rocking across the ages on their peeling front porches, of our grandmothers dressed in aprons like altar robes, and, when we return to the old neighborhood, perhaps over-hearing echoes even of ourselves.

Will Scheffer

At the opening of **ALIEN BOY**, the young Jewish protagonist, dolled up in a sailor suit, a becoming pick-up costume, waits to embark upon his life's voyage—preferably in the arms of some Aryan-stud role model. In the background, there is "a nuclear bomb exploding," the calamitous scream of the nuclear family detonating into unrecognizable molecules. The play's unspoken mantra, "Never Forget" also echoes quietly behind the boy's feverish obsession to do just that: *Forget at All Costs*. He dreams of space ships and lovers from the galaxy where he "belongs," where he at long last will be embraced for the extra terrestrial he might well be.

Alienation is a naturally unnatural condition in Will Scheffer's world. The bar mitzvah candidate wears his mother's heels while incinerating the names of ancestors who perished at Auschwitz. The shrink he picks from the yellow pages of his white New Jersey suburb, Dr. Casey (à la the TV idol), turns out to be handsome enough, but black. The second generation Jew denies his own heritage and hurls the N-word at the analyst when he betrays him. We don't learn our protagonist's name because his identity is constantly in flux; his hostility is omnidirectional, aimed everywhere including himself. There is a name for history, for his parents, for his ancestors, but not for him in the present. The plastic polymers of his experimental life finally conflagrate and, from the ashes, emerges a world that waits for lies and self-deception to expire.

Christopher Durang

O'Brien takes refuge on a tropical island to forget his failed marriage in Durang's **KITTY THE WAITRESS.** He stumbles upon an idyllic French bistro where amnesia is the signature sauce ladled heartily over the special-ités de la maison. There's a reminiscent whiff from Shaw's strand cafe in *You Never Can Tell*, where the principals gather to escape the past and instead run headlong into it. O'Brien exhorts his pretty French waitress to correct her seductive posture and "Pull your private parts in." But it is precisely the private parts of life that will not be girdled or long repressed. Old postures reassert themselves; a man's core predilections never vacation in the Caribbean; life's baggage is not so easily stowed away.

Given a wildly kaleidoscopic range of menu specialties, O'Brien reverts to his Midwestern adolescent palate and orders a rare hamburger—his only nod to the local cuisine being a side order of French fries. O'Brien can no more adjust his palate than he can his nature. It is at this point that the raison d'etre of the cafe itself begins to morph, and Kitty screams out in purest Canarsien: "Hey, Mario! Gimme a Number 42, with grease and slaw, bloody!" The fantasy succumbs to a world of consequence again. And like the wine that Kitty cannot uncork, O'Brien finds it hard to breathe; his own life remains uncorked and untried.

Joyce Carol Oates

Our culture is saturated with self-induced states of bourgeois synchronici-ty. Oceans of mantras on "How to Make the World Come to You" cascade off chain-store end caps. Prime Time Gurus beat us into self-realization: In order to receive our renewed redecorated Destiny, we need only "put it out there" for the universe to register our wishes like newlyweds registering for a pattern of dinnerware at Bloomingdales. Fashionable celebrity Buddhists giddy with solipsistic matchmaking reread the Zen of Self and fall in love all over again.

But what of the lives that were never in synch? What becomes of those disowned by Fate, those who haven't learned the secret of networking at the Princeton Club? Joyce Carol Oates' Woman was clasped briefly to the breast only to be perpetually pushed away. The Woman survives her life but never commences it; she is alive now that her nine blood siblings and her blood mother are dead, but she can never advance out of the girlhood that was denied her. Starting many subjects in a faltering fairy-tale cadence, she finishes each one with the inescapable reprise: "When I was a little girl my mother gave me away."

Arthur Kopit

Dante's über resonant lines, which initiate Kopit's mock epic, constitute the poetic scrim behind which all superheroes must labor. Every regeneration of the superheroic tale delivers up a new translation of that savage forest. Kopit reminds us that new episodes are but slightly revised approximations of that hell. Chad stands on the same threshold as all the Herculean brethren who have dared to pierce the dark veil of the nether realm. He wields a new techno-fab sword to battle a cousin-once-removed from the Red Knight's arch-nemesis. We stand on an old battlefield in Kopit's play, aching from old wounds.

There is a mock-Churchillian quality to Chad's muffled exhortation: "Dongivvup." We have been thrust into a galaxy of raw perseverance where even the corpses, buoyant with bloating, itch for renovation to fight another day. To endure the world's indefatigable evil requires an innocence no number of clashes can tarnish, or perhaps a noggin into which no sense can be knocked. On the other hand, here there really is no pain in gain. Castration is but a mere interlude between passionate bouts. Lose your penis, and choose among six new styles and sizes from the cosmic erector set. Apocalypse is merely the rumbling soundtrack. Yet the wounds in **CHAD CURTISS—LOST AGAIN** are old because we are each an ad-hoc assemblage of dead men fallen in the battle of our fathers.

The form of Kopit's play is itself a bit of castrate-and-paste. There is a surreal Gyntian quality to the hypermorphic characters, a yearning toward Gilbert & Sullivan when Verdi puts down his baton. The Pythons would envy Kopit's majestically sophomoric anticlimax to the Grail quest. The consummation of the play's action perhaps says it all: "To Be Continued."

Leslie Ayvazian

This is a mother's salute to the sun in a world beclouded by prejudice and trauma. The mother in **DEAF DAY** does not try to make the world go away. She does not disperse, diminish, or disguise it. She does not cover her own ears to life's harsher vibes. She declines even to demonize her son's hearing tormenters. Instead, she invites her deaf son into the world's wondrous tumult where he will never be totally at home. She pries the heavy-lidded world open with invitations to the teeter-totter, a fulcrum where he might temporarily find balance and even a moment of mastery. She's a master at balance herself inculcating sympathy in her son even for the world's impatience and frustration. She escorts him to the playground, but she cannot ride the slide for him nor deflect the bullying from his hearing peers. At best she can sit on a nearby bench, a world away. And as we take the seat on the bench next to her, we are offered a hearing aid for the non-hearing impaired; a vouchsafement of grace for those who take our blessings for granted. As in other plays in this volume, language comes neither easily nor naturally.

The mother's cheerleading "Rise and Shine" is optimistic but pragmatic, the only prayer for wholeness possible in an incomplete and incomprehensible universe. The play is practically bare of props. There are no materialistic fixes; no slick wands from the Sharper Image catalog to mediate the silence. Mother and son appear to be the entire stripped-down family; the absence of father or siblings makes the mother-son bond oddly delicate. He is bound entirely to her and yet if they are to prevail she must ultimately surrender him to that harsh world. One can only speculate that the Mother's great wisdom has come at its own price in her own journey through life's rough-and-tumble jungle gym.

Beth Henley

Beth Henley renders a heartbreaking fairy tale, a grotesque de Maupassant, a noble love story debased by greed and disgraced by savage desire. **SISTERS OF THE WINTER MADRIGAL** is a drama of degeneration about a mythic world capable of natural purity and piety but which instead mutilates itself and descends into bestiality and sacrilege. It is peopled by a dismembered tribe, alienated from their roots, quadfurcated by schizophrenic urges. How does one proclaim love, then measure and cherish it, in a world antithetical to its soul? How does one articulate ideas that one can just barely grasp? **SISTERS** is also a play about courage and dignity in the face of tyranny and the many faces of sacrifice arrayed on the altar of love. Perhaps above all, Henley probes what finally satisfies our deepest human cravings—that which we must crave to be human.

Not through the ministrations of Iloveyou.com does Calilah, the nearly-mute orphan of Jonah the Cow Herder, plight her troth with her garrulous suitor, Stephan, the shoemaker. Their pledge is sealed not by any earthly trinket but by the brooch of the brightest little star in the sky. There is no store-bought emblem; no logo from Tiffany's broadcasts the eternity of their bond. Calilah knows the direction of the Tiffany line; her sister, Taretta, the town whore, receives payment in such tarnished currency every night from one husband or another who avidly recycles his wedding ring and other symbols of undying affection for a hot night in a strange sack. The dramatic concatenation of the two sisters' fate links one to bondage and putrefaction and the other to an exhilarating bond of emancipation. Neither Calilah nor Stephan escapes the indecencies of tyranny, but their choices live on in this cautionary drama for twenty-first-century America.

Paul Kuritz

A New England physician moves his delicate wife to an old house for a transient stay while their own home is being renovated. Rather than the suite of rooms that opens out onto the landscaped piazza, Dr. John installs his frail wife in the former nursery, an attic where the windows are barred and the floors and woodwork are scarred and ravaged from the antics of rowdy boys who years ago attended school there. The physician's wife becomes increasingly his patient, and her life increasingly becomes a medical case to be cured. Sequestered at the top of the stairs, remote from her society and even from her own child—who her husband has put under the care of his sister—the mother keeps society with the only world not denied her: Her writer's imagination engages the ancient yellow wallpaper, which appears to undulate with Protean characters and plot like a moving Rorschach test.

The young mother locked into the nursery without her child gives birth to fantasies about commingled lives, new and old. The inanimate wallpaper begins to assert a karma of its own that cannot be suppressed, its eyes and hands—which first follow the young writer—soon reach out into the skin of its ailing inhabitant. The doctor infantalizes his wife and challenges her sanity in this bold precursor to Vincent Price. But the tactile and sensuous reality of the yellow wallpaper supplants her own, until the woman's limbic organs eventually revive with new alertness and vitality. Draughts from the past now sweep through the house and lock out the physician—rejecting his patent cures as well as his patent lies.

Neena Beber

Life is a setup for a familiar joke. A doctor tells his patient: "We have good news and bad news." The bad news is that Franz Kafka is nearly dead. Felice, Kafka's beloved, requests a cosmic waiver but is rebuffed by the doctor, a specialist in buffoonery, a figure of commedia, an authoritative fool. Death is a game that permits no substitutions or time-outs. Ultimately, the bad news becomes indistinguishable from the good. The life-or-death struggle degenerates into an incestuous children's game where, since everything is interchangeable, nothing endures, except the inexorable dance of Death.

"Switch places" is the play's reprise in the game of musical chairs Beber's characters play at. No one escapes these roles and no one plays them for long. Alexander Pope's diagnosis seems apt: "The disease that is my life." "I couldn't find a soul," the exasperated Felice declares. In Kafka's final institutional throes, why is it that we are not surprised?

Laura Shaine Cunningham

It's midnight at the Depression Clinic when only two novitiates turn up for the advertised free therapy. In a realistic play there would be thousands of manic Manhattanites queuing up. To score free experimental antidepressants! That's as uplifting as life gets for a real-life depressive. But since depression is in the mind of the beholder, Cunningham's play settles back into its own absurd collective head.

Liv, the female patient, wants, of course, to die, and Mo, naturally, wants nothing more than less of everything. These are people whose metro fare cards expired after trips they never took. Mo, who only sucks the filter on his cigarette, needs to be ignited. After years of abandonment by his parents, he's followed suit by abandoning himself. The voice in Liv's head that urges her to "Jump!" may have the right trajectory. Liv has lived a life of tentative commitment, conditional acceptance. The only thing that stops her from suicide is that she has "no follow-through." Well, suicide may be going a bit far, but any path might be preferable to the endless loop of self-abnegation she trudges now.

As the treatment progresses, the poisonous roots of the depression rather than narrowing and dispersing, spread and deepen. Mental disorder becomes a worldwide phenomenon and any state other than societal psychosis seems perverse. Before the session is over, the physicians themselves succumb to the emotional undertow. Dr. Obolenski, sex goddess and famous researcher, admits "it is all hopeless…nothing can remedy despair." But the doctor's gloom is premature; once the new Euphoria Brand of Starbucks kicks in, patients and physicians break down their individual silos of despair and "swirl into dance."

Donna de Matteo

Much of New York City's Queens borough government becomes complicit in the cover-up of a fatally botched abortion. Responsibility ricochets from Billy, the privileged young man who impregnates his girlfriend at their senior prom, to the rigid mores of the '50s, to the nepotism that prevails in local government, to the boy's parents.

Billy's life has been one long premature ejaculation. It's all over before he or Kathy got started. The young man made the age-old pitch to his date at the Holy Cross senior prom about proving her undying love in the only way seventeen-year-olds in 1957 (or many a year before or since) understand. He never expects Kathy to swing for the fences; he is simply obliged by the code of senior proms to get it over her plate. Billy's script goes haywire because Billy was not prepared for acquiescence. A snap, a fumble, and a clumsy pop later, the dramatic die is cast. From then on, Billy and Kathy are entangled in a web of B-movie scenarios that ultimately crash inside the new Ford Fairlane 500 the young man received as a graduation present. Billy will never get a chance to drive his shiny new gift from the Elmhurst Emergency Room parking lot.

We are in a skillfully wrought melodrama with Billy on the hot seat, squirming as the defense attorney hired by his influential father privately prosecutes him for the crime before he even gets to the courtroom. Billy's inept staging of the girl's demise is cut to ribbons by the sharp attorney. The dramatist sets up a situation that demands judgment and then powerfully resists casting the first stone. The judge, father to the boy, authority figure to the community, and accomplice to the cover up, remains a powerful presence despite of and because of, his absence. In fact, there are many judges here. Only the writer is not one of them. Who's to blame? Billy is clearly guilty. But who's not to blame?

Lives of the Saints

David Ives

David Ives

David Ives was born in Chicago and educated at the Yale School of Drama. A former Guggenheim Foundation Fellow in playwriting, he is probably best known for his evening of one-act comedies called *All in the Timing*. His short plays are collected in two anthologies, *All in the Timing* (Vintage) and *Time Flies* (Grove). His full-length theatre works are available in *Polish Joke and Other Plays* (Grove). He is also the author of two young-adult novels, *Monsieur Eek* and *Scrib*. Most recently, he translated Georges Feydeau's classic French farce *A Flea in Her Ear*. He lives in New York City with his wife, Martha.

characters

EDNA   Nancy Opel

FLO   Anne O'Sullivan

ASSISTANTS   Arnie Burton, Bradford Cover, Danton Stone

• • •

[*Totally bare stage—which will remain totally bare till noted. EDNA enters up right and FLO enters up left as if through swinging doors we do not see. There is a momentary burst of distant church funeral music as they enter, as if we are overhearing music from where they came from. EDNA and FLO wear ancient flowered housedresses, spotless aprons, and loudly flapping, flattened slippers. Each carries something in her arms which we do not see. They cross passing each other. Chicago accents.*]

FLO   I got da candle'ss. You got da doilese?

EDNA   I got da St. Stanislas Kostka doilese.

FLO   Oll do da utensil'ss.

EDNA   Oll do da plate'ss.

[*They exit on opposite sides, again to that momentary burst of church music, but reenter immediately.*]

Opp, dat's da wrong side.

FLO   Opp, dat's da wrong side.

EDNA   What'm I tinkin…

FLO   What'm I tinkin…

[*They recross and exit and we hear the offstage noise of a hundred rattled utensils and a hundred clattering plates. EDNA and FLO reenter and again we hear that momentary burst of church music.*]

EDNA Okay, so we put out utensil'ss…

FLO An we put out da plate'ss…

EDNA Da candle'ss have ta be lit.

FLO An' we got da St. Stanislas Kostka doilese.

[EDNA *heads counterclockwise,* FLO *clockwise as if around a large table we do not see.* EDNA *goes to a stove at left that we do not see, and* FLO *turns on an invisible "hand-mixer" and we hear "VRRRRRRR!"* EDNA *taps an invisible "wooden spoon" on the side of an invisible "pot" and we hear "TAP, TAP, TAP." Then the two women move down center where side by side each woman turns a "faucet" and they wash their hands under water we don't see, but which we hear running.*]

EDNA Now dat was a very nice funeral.

FLO Wasn't dat a beautyful funeral.

EDNA I wouldn't mind having dat.

FLO I wouldn't mind having dat for my funeral.

EDNA But I will tell you a song I don not want sung at my funeral. Da t'eme from "Da Phantom of the Opera" is not appropriate.

FLO An' not "Is That All There Is" needer.

EDNA Omm traditional, Flo.

FLO Edna, Omm traditional, too.

[*We hear the "DING!" of a kitchen timer.*]

EDNA Opp, dere's da cake.

[*They each turn a "faucet" and the water sound stops.*]

FLO   Oll check da jello moldss.

EDNA   Oll check da cake.

[*Moving around the invisible table,* EDNA *circles left,* FLO *circles right.*]

FLO   Ha we doin' fer time?

EDNA   We got until da cemetery an back.

FLO   Plenny a time.

EDNA   Plenny a time.

[EDNA *opens an "oven door" which we do not see and we hear a "CREAK!"* FLO *opens an invisible "refrigerator door."*]

Fi'e more minutes.

FLO   Fi'e more minutes.

[*"CREAK!" "BANG!"*]

EDNA   [*Pointing to a "dish" on a "sideboard" we don't see.*]
Okay, sa we did da patayta salad…

FLO   [*Pointing to another "dish" on a "sideboard."*] Da green salad…

EDNA   [*Pointing elsewhere.*] Fruit salad.

FLO   [*Pointing elsewhere.*] Cole slaw.

EDNA   [*Pointing to a "table" at center we do not see.*] Der's da apple slices.

FLO   [*Pointing to "table."*] Nut clusters.

EDNA   [*Pointing to "table."*] Cheese cake.

FLO   [*Pointing to "oven."*] Pond cake, crumb cake, angel food.

EDNA [*Pointing to "sideboard."*] Krooshcheeki.

FLO [*Pointing elsewhere.*] Kolachki.

EDNA [*Pointing to "table."*] Krooler'ss.

FLO [*Pointing to "refrigerator."*] Jello.

EDNA [*Pointing to "stove."*] An prune'ss.

FLO For twelve people?

EDNA I tink it's enough.

FLO [*Heading for "sideboard" at right.*] Der used to be pot holders down here with St. Damien an da lepers.

EDNA [*Heading for "stove" at left.*] Odda know what happened to dose lepers.

[EDNA *stirs a "pot" we don't see while shaking in "salt" and we hear the "SPRINKLE, SPRINKLE." FLO at the "counter" turns on an invisible "handmixer" and we hear its motor: "VRRRRRR!" EDNA taps the "pot" with a "wooden spoon": "TAP, TAP, TAP."*]

EDNA Plus we got da sossitch.

FLO Der's da sossitch.

[*"SPRINKLE, SPRINKLE!" "VRRRRRR!" "TAP, TAP, TAP!"*]

EDNA Der's da chicken with Campbell's mushroom soup.

FLO Der's da perogi.

EDNA Da perogi, da gawoomki.

[*"SPRINKLE, SPRINKLE!" "VRRRRRR!" TAP, TAP, TAP!"*]

FLO Der's kapoosta.

EDNA Da rollss, da bunss en da bread.

FLO And da Polish glazed ham.

[*"SPRINKLE." "VRRRRRR!" "TAP, TAP, TAP."*]

EDNA For twelve people…?

FLO I tink it's enough.

> [FLO *carries the "bowl" she was mixing to the "table" at center.*]

EDNA Don't put dad der, Flo, it's dirty.

FLO Is it dirty?

EDNA Yeah, it's dirty.

> [EDNA *sweeps "crumbs" from the "table" and we hear the sweeping sound.*]
>
> Oll do da poddered sugar.

FLO Oll do da nuts.

[EDNA *goes to unseen "high cabinets" at left. FLO to a bank of "lowdrawers" at left.*]

EDNA Okay, wurr's da poddered sugar…

FLO Okay, wurr's da nuts…

EDNA Poddered sugar…

> [EDNA *opens a "cabinet." We hear a "SQUEAK!"*]

FLO Nuts…

[FLO *opens an unseen "drawer": "CREAK!" EDNA closes the "cabinet": "BANG!"*]

EDNA Poddered sugar…

[*"SQUEAK!"*]

FLO Nuts…

[*"CREAK!" "BANG!"*]

EDNA Fodder Tom says to me Edna wouldja do a funeral breakfast fer Mary, I couldn't find nobody.

FLO I say to um, Fodder I cooked so many meals in dis church bazement…

EDNA I'm happy to.

[*"SQUEAK!"*]

FLO …I might's well live in dis church bazement.

EDNA I says, Mary'll need some substenance.

FLO Edna and me'll throw somethin together.

EDNA [*Finding it.*] Opp! Da poddered sugar.

FLO Opp! Da nuts.

[*They close "cabinet" and "drawer": "BANG!" "BANG!" The two women go to the "table" at center.*]

EDNA O, da tings dat Mary has been t'rough.

FLO O, da tragedy innat family.

EDNA Just terrible.

FLO Just terrible.

[*We hear "SIFT, SIFT" as* EDNA *sifts unseen powdered sugar and a "GRIND, GRIND" as* FLO *turns the crank of an unseen nut grinder.*]

An' you know Barney didn't leave her nuttin.

EDNA I always tought Barney was gonna come to a bad end wid alla dat drinkin.

FLO Run over by his own lawn mower.

EDNA Just terrible.

FLO Just terrible.

[*"SPRINKLE, SPRINKLE." "GRIND, GRIND." During this, the back wall of the stage opens up and we see two stagehands who are at a table doing all the sound effects.* EDNA *and* FLO *do not acknowledge them.*]

EDNA I'm prayin to St. Jude fer Mary.

FLO Patron saint a lost causes.

EDNA Jude'll bring her somethin.

FLO You remember what St. Jude did fer me when I had piles.

EDNA He brought you dat special ointment.

FLO A miracle. [*"SPRINKLE, SPRINKLE." "GRIND, GRIND."*]

EDNA Ya know when Joe died Mary made me sixteen ponds a perogi.

[EDNA *opens "cabinet": "SQUEAK" and puts away "powdered sugar can," then closes "cabinet": "BANG."*]

FLO When Stosh died Mary gay'me a twenty-two-pond turkey.

[FLO *opens "drawer"—"CREAK"—puts away "nuts" and closes "drawer": "BANG."*]

EDNA   So der's justice in da world.

FLO   So der's some justice.

[*They move down center and turn unseen "squeaky faucets."*]

EDNA   Too bad we couldn't go ta da cemetery.

FLO   For Mary's sake.

[*The stage assistants upstage pour water into a bucket as EDNA and FLO wash their hands under the invisible water.*]

EDNA   St. Casimir's my favorite cemetery, too.

FLO   Just beautyful.

EDNA   Da way dey take care a da grave'ss der.

FLO   Da grave'ss are always like noo.

EDNA   An da bat'rooms.

FLO   Spotless.

EDNA   I just pre-ordered my casket from dat place in Blue Island.

FLO   I got my casket. Didja get da blue coffin wit satin?

EDNA   I got pink wit chiffon.

FLO   Just beautyful.

EDNA   Just beautyful.

[*They turn "faucets" and the water sound stops.*]

FLO   I bought some patayta chips.

EDNA   I bought some taco chips.

[*They pick up invisible chip bags, while the assistants upstage crinkle real cellophane bags.*]

FLO   Patayta chips…

EDNA   Taco chips…

FLO   Patayta chips…

EDNA   Taco chips…

   [*They stop. The crinkling stops.*]

FLO   Ya tink chips are appropriate fer a funeral breakfast?

EDNA   Maybe not for breakfast.

FLO   Not for breakfast.

[*"DING!" of a kitchen timer.*]

EDNA and **FLO**   Opp!

FLO   Ya wanna check da jello?

EDNA   Ya wanna check da cake?

   [FLO *moves left.* EDNA *moves right.*]

FLO   I was gonna make duck blood soup wit raisins and dumplings. But you know da problem wit makin duck blood soup no more.

EDNA   You can't find no duck blood.

FLO   Der's no duck blood.

[*"CREAKS," as* EDNA *and* FLO *open "stove" and "refrigerator" doors.*]

EDNA   My ma use ta kill da ducks herself in da ga-rotch.

FLO   You know it's not da killin.

EDNA   It's when dey urinate all over you.

FLO   Just terrible.

EDNA   Just terrible.

FLO   Cake's done.

EDNA   Jello's done.

> [*They close "stove" and "refrigerator" and we hear: "CREAK!" "BANG!"*]

FLO   It's da same t'ing wit makin pickled pigs' feet.

EDNA   Der's no feet.

[FLO *sprinkles "salt"*—*"SPRINKLE, SPRINKLE"*—*then taps a "wooden spoon" on the "pot" : "TAP, TAP, TAP." EDNA shakes an invisible "whipped cream can" and we hear the shaking can.*]

I toldja I lost doze feet I bought in Blue Island.

FLO   Did you pray to St. Ant'ny?

EDNA   I prayed to St. Ant'ny, two days later I found um.

FLO   Were da feet in de izebox?

EDNA   Da feet were in de izebox alla time.

FLO   [*Sighs.*]

EDNA   [*Sighs.*]

[*"SPRINKLE, SPRINKLE, SPRINKLE"*—*"SHAKE, SHAKE"*—*"TAP, TAP, TAP."*]

Wit' da whip' cream, should I do rosettes or da squiggle'ss?

FLO   I tink rosettes.

EDNA   Rosettes…? Fine.

FLO   [*"SPRINKLE"—"SHAKE."*] Or maybe rosettes in da middle…

EDNA   …squiggle'ss on da side.

FLO   Squiggle'ss on da side.

[*"PFFFLLLL!"—*EDNA *sprays invisible whipped cream on an unseen cake. Then* FLO *taps and* EDNA *sprays, and soon the rhythm of this has developed into something like the "Beer Barrel Polka," and they're humming along with it, really getting into it, "banging" on the "pots," "table" and "stove" we don't see like a two-woman band. When they stop:*]

EDNA   [*Sighs.*]

FLO   [*Sighs.*]

EDNA   Ya know Fodder Tom tol'me a joke today.

FLO   O yeah?

>   [*"PFFFLLLL."*]

EDNA   What's it say onna bottom a Polish Coca-Cola bottles?

FLO   What's it say onna bottom a Polish Coca-Cola bottles…

EDNA   Onna bottom a Polish Coca-Cola bottles.

FLO   I give up.

EDNA   "Open Udder End."

>   [*They laugh. "SPRINKLE, SPRINKLE, SPRINKLE." "PFFFLLLL"— "BANG, BANG, BANG."*]

EDNA   In Polish, I mean.

FLO Oh sure.

[*"PFFFLLLL"…* EDNA *carries "whipped cream" back to "refrigerator" and "puts it inside."*]

EDNA He says to me, Mrs. Pavletski I hope yer not offended, I say to um Fodder, when yer Polish—what can offend you?

FLO When my Stosh tried to burn a wasps' nest outa the garotch an' burnt da garotch down—that was a Polish joke.

[*Sighs.*]

EDNA [*Sighs.*] Well, I guess we got a minute.

FLO I guess w'er done till da funeral gets back. Yeah, I guess w'er ready.

[*The wall behind them closes up and the sound effects people disappear from sight as the two women circle the "table," pointing to "things" to make sure they're ready. Each woman then pulls out a "chair" we don't see on the side of the table. Just as the women are about to sit down on nothing, two stagehands run in with chairs, and hold them for the women, who sit down without acknowledging the presence of the stagehands.*]

EDNA Flo, you always make da best apple slices. Wh'er's da forks…

[*She reaches for a fork we don't see and a stagehand holds one out. She takes it without acknowledging the stagehand.*]

FLO Well, Edna, you make da best angel food. Wh'er's da forks…

[*FLO reaches for a fork we don't see, and the other stagehand hands her one. The women reach their forks toward plates that aren't there, and two other stagehands run in with plates of dessert. Without acknowledging the stagehands, each of the women takes a small piece of cake.*]

EDNA Oll just take a small one.

FLO   Oll just take a little piece, dey'll never notice.

EDNA   Flo.

FLO   Look at dat. Just delicious…

EDNA   Flo.

FLO   Odda know how ya do it, Ed.

EDNA   Flo, when I die, will ya do my funeral breakfast?

[*Pause.*]

FLO   Sure I will, Ed.

EDNA   Will you make yer apple slices?

FLO   Sure, Ed.

EDNA   An will ya make sure da choir don't sing dat damn song?

FLO   Sure I will, Ed.

EDNA   Thank you, Flo.

FLO   An if I go first, will you do my funeral breakfast?

EDNA   You know I will, Flo. I could make duck blood soup.

FLO   Don't bodder with da duck blood. Angel food is fine.

> [FLO *takes* EDNA'*s hand and squeezes it, holding onto it. A radiant cone of light bathes the two women, and two doves appear, one over each of their heads. Without surprise.*]

Edna, ya know you got a dove over yer head?

EDNA   [*Without surprise.*] You know you got one, too, Flo?

FLO   Yeah, well.

[*They reach for another dessert, and a stagehand steps in with a bowl heaped with fruit. Each woman takes an apple and polishes it on her dress.*]

FLO   "Open Udder End."

EDNA   "Open Udder End…" 'At's—real—good.

[*They laugh gently.*]

EDNA and **FLO** [*Sigh.*]

[*The lights fade.*]

• • •

Alien Boy

Will Scheffer

Will Scheffer

Will Scheffer is an award-winning playwright and screenwriter. His plays have been produced and/or workshopped across the country and at such theatres as: Playwright's Horizons, Naked Angels, the Actors Studio (member), Ensemble Studio Theater (member), and the Public Theater. He was selected to be one of the members of the Joseph Papp Public Theater's First Emerging Playwright's Lab in 1994 and, in the same year, was chosen by the HBO New Writer's Project as one of ten new writers of exceptional promise.

In 1997 he wrote his first screenplay, *In the Gloaming*, starring Glenn Close and directed by Christopher Reeve for HBO. It was nominated for five Emmys, including Best Television Movie; nominated for a WGA Writing Award; and won the Cable Ace Writing Award and Christopher Award. That year he was listed as one of *Variety*'s Rising Writers to Watch.

With his writing partner, Mark V. Olsen, he created the original HBO series *Big Love* and *Mailman*, a feature film adaptation of the novel for Paramount. He wrote *Howard Hughes' Last Flight* for the FX television network; *The Pact* starring Megan Mullally and Juliet Stevenson, *Honor Roll Bonnie and Clyde* for Lifetime Television; and *Home* for HBO Films.

In 2000, he adapted and produced his play *Easter* as an independent film with his partner, Mark V. Olsen, for their production company, Anima Sola Productions, and filmed on location in Nebraska. *Easter* has won awards for Best Feature Film and Best Actress. It was screened at the prestigious Santa Barbara Film Festival and made its Nebraska premiere at the Hastings Museum, where Mr. Scheffer and Mr. Olsen received keys to the city and became Honorary Citizens of Nebraska.

Theatre: *Easter* (Naked Angels, published by Dramatists Play Service); *Alien Boy* (Ensemble Studio Theatre Marathon 2000); *Tennessee and Me* (E.S.T. Marathon '97, Tennessee Williams Festival '98); *Bel Canto* (E.S.T. Marathon '96); *Falling Man* (E.S.T Marathon '94, selected for Penguin/Viking's *The Actors' Book of Gay and Lesbian Plays*); *Multiple Personality* (New Works Now: Joseph Papp Public Theater).

[*Sousa march blares as the lights fade. Lights up on a boy in a sailor suit.*]

ALIEN BOY   Today I am thirteen.

[*Sound: A nuclear bomb exploding.*]

I don't want to be thirteen. I have always yearned to be older than my years. Therefore I have been described as a precocious child. I drink coffee. I smoke cigarettes. I use the words: masturbatory, ennui, and existential—liberally in conversation. But today I am thirteen. I am wearing my sailor suit. I come down here often in my sailor suit, to the Howard Johnson's in Bloomfield, New Jersey, and I wait. I wait for a man to come and take me away, away from this childhood that I do not belong in. A blonde man who is muscular and bold, I have seen him on TV. He will teach me how to be athletic and brave. He will give structure and meaning to my life. He will hold me in the dark. Just we two. I wait and wait. But he never seems to come.

[BOY *lights a cigarette.*]

I was supposed to be Bar Mitzvahed today. But I told my mother I wouldn't go. I told her I had decided I didn't want to be Jewish anymore. My mother was distraught. "You can't just decide you don't want to be Jewish anymore," she said. I told her again, "I don't want to be Jewish." "Why don't you want to be Jewish?" she asked me. "In the street, children throw pennies at me, they call me Jew Bagel, in an age when it is possible for us to choose our own destiny, I have decided I don't want to go through life with the particular disadvantage of being a Jew. I want to be Blonde and Handsome like the men on TV. I want to drive a Volkswagen." "Over my dead body, you'll drive a Volkswagen. This wouldn't be happening if your father were alive." "He's not alive," I said, "he's dead!" My mother took a Valium and locked herself in her bedroom.

[*Sound: a door slamming.*]

My father was a Jew.

[BOY *lights another cigarette.*]

He came to America during World War Two. He was—an Alien.

[*Music: "Psycho."*]

He left behind his mother, sister, his first wife, and a son. They died at Auschwitz. I have here their names, as listed by the Red Cross. Rebecca, Betsy, Rachel, and the son, Wolf, who was shoveled into an oven on the day of his thirteenth birthday in 1943.

[*Sound: fire. Combustion.*]

[*He burns the names of his relatives with flash paper.*]

I never got along with my father. He spoke with a heavy foreign accent. He was thin and pale and European, not at all like the men on TV. One day I was walking around the house in my mother's high heels and my father caught me. He slapped me and told me: "I never want you to walk in high heels again. Soon you will be thirteen, you will be Bar Mitzvahed, soon you will be a man." "I don't want to be a man," I told him. "*You're* a man, I wish you were dead." The next year he died of lung cancer. Now I wear my mother's high heels whenever she's not home.

[*He puts on high heels. "I Feel Pretty" from* West Side Story *plays as the* ALIEN BOY *twirls.*]

I turn up the music from *West Side Story* and I twirl my baton.

[*When the lyrics reach: "I feel pretty, and witty, and gay"… The music stops with a screech and horror music fades in.*]

Last night after my mother had cooked me a Swanson's frozen TV dinner, I was reading *Everything You Always Wanted to Know About Sex but Were Afraid to Ask* by David Rueben, M.D., and I quote:

VOICEOVER   "Male Homosexuality is a condition in which men have a driving emotional and sexual interest in other men. Because of the anatomical and physiological limitations involved, there are some formidable obstacles to overcome. In the process they often transform themselves into part-time women. They don women's clothes, wear makeup, adopt feminine mannerisms, and occasionally even try to rearrange their bodies along feminine lines."

ALIEN BOY   I don't want to be a homosexual. Until last night I didn't know I was one. I knew I was different, but I didn't think there was a name for it. I knew I liked to wear my mother's slip. I knew I liked to wrestle with my friend Nicky Sabatini, and I knew I didn't mind losing. I knew I liked to rub against the sofa watching Monty Hall on *Let's Make a Deal* and the cowboys on *Bonanza*. But then I read this:

VOICEOVER   "Some of the more routine items that find their way into the gastrointestinal systems of homosexuals via the exit are pens, pencils, lipsticks, combs, pop bottles, ladies' electric shavers, and enough other items to stock a small department store."

[*Sound: electric shaver.*]

ALIEN BOY   I definitely don't want to be a homosexual. One day, after we finish wrestling, Nicky Sabatini tells me that there is a movie called *Boys in the Band*, about Homos. I decide that I must see this movie, that perhaps it will shed light on this condition, this horrible thing that is me. I ask my mother to take me. I need her to take me because children are not permitted to see it unless accompanied by their legal guardian. "What's it about?" she asks.

"About a group of musicians." "Why do you want to see it so bad?" "Because as you know, I am learning how to play the tuba, and my motivation is already failing because it's so hard to carry it back and forth to school."

My mother agrees to take me because she would do anything to encourage my musicality. We go to the Royal Theater that night for the eight o'clock show.

[*Sousa music.*]

When we get to the theater the woman who sells tickets will not let me in. She says the movie is unsuitable for children my age. I demand to see the manager. "It's illegal," I say, "what you're doing." The lady calls the manager. He is from a foreign country. He can't believe my mother would take me to see such a movie. "Do you know what it's about?" he asks her. "Musicians," she answers. He pulls her away from me and talks to her in hushed foreign tones. When she returns she tells me we can't enter, "I'm sorry, why don't we go to the Welmont Theater to see *Snow White and the Seven Dwarfs*? I start to throw a fit. "It's illegal, what they're doing," I say again. "I'm going to write a letter." My mother takes me across the street to Woolworth's and offers to buy me a Hot Wheels set. "I don't want it," I say. I hold out until she buys me a GI Joe doll. She takes me home and makes me Jell-O.

The next evening I convince my mother that it is her civic responsibility to allow me to see *Boys in the Band*. "This is America," I remind her. "It's a free country." Finally, she agrees to take me to a theater in New York City, where we have no trouble attaining admittance.

[*The lights dim. Music: "Heatwave."*]

As we sit in the darkness, I nervously eat a pack of Goobers and Raisinets. My mother fidgets and allows a pack of Eskimo Pies to melt uneaten onto her ecru pants suit. We watch together in horror as a group of genuine homosexuals complain about their mothers and dance together in a conga line—and as we watch, a subtle electricity flows back and forth between my mother and myself, an unmistakable unspoken acknowledgement that now we both understand why I wanted to see this movie. When we leave the theater we are silent, in tacit agreement that we will not mention the horrible truth, that somewhere deep inside of us, we have both in this moment come to know.

[*Sci-fi music plays. Lights flash outside the window.*]

That night I have a disturbing dream. Outside my window I see strange lights. A spaceship lands and a robot man descends from its steps and comes into my bedroom, He is very blonde and looks like my GI Joe doll and the devastatingly handsome Nazis I have seen in war films. He comes to my bed and takes me on his lap. He looks very cold like metal but when he touches me his skin is hot. He holds me in his hot arms. He says that: "You must tell me that you love me." I look into his blonde eyes. I start to form the words I love you. "I… Love…" I wake up screaming.

[*Sound: a horror movie scream.*]

It's two in the morning. In the *Boys in the Band*, all the Homosexuals had psychiatrists. I creep into the kitchen and go for the Yellow Pages. I look under the letter P. I find the names of all psychiatrists in Bloomfield. Both of them. Dr. Kaplan and Dr. Casey. I choose Dr. Casey, because he sounds more attractive. I write him a brief letter:

"Dear Dr. Casey:

I think I am a homosexual. I have no money. I cannot tell my mother. Please help me. I want to be cured."

I find a stamp in my mother's pocketbook. For the rest of the night I dream of my doctor. The one who will save me. The man I've been waiting for.

The next day while carrying my tuba, I mail the letter to my doctor. The boys at school have stopped calling me Jewboy and have begun to call me pussy and faggot. I now dress in work boots and flannel shirts to disguise myself. Anxious weeks pass as daily, I run home after school to check the mailbox. Every night I stay awake until 4, praying to the God I do not believe in to save me from my sordid fate. Then one day a letter arrives addressed to me.

[*Vicki Carr singing: "Dear God It Must Be Him." The* ALIEN BOY *clutches the letter to his chest and opens it, his heart pounding.*]

He will see me one week from today in his office. I am filled with excruciating anticipation. The week passes quickly, and on the day of our assignation I run from school to the bus that will take me to my hero. I have dressed in my argyle shirt and socks, corduroy bell-bottoms and platform shoes, tempting derogatory slurs from the boys in gym class, but I don't care, I am reckless with expectation.

I arrive at the address of Dr. Casey's office. I ring the bell and am buzzed into a small waiting room. "I'm here to see Dr. Casey," I say to the secretary with a hint of pride. As she knocks suspiciously on the doctor's door I look around his office. I am disappointed to find other people here. The secretary returns and ushers me into Dr. Casey's office. Suddenly, as I am face to face with the man who knows my secret, I realize why I have felt vaguely disoriented since arriving. Dr. Casey is a black person, like his secretary and the people in the waiting room. I am momentarily unable to process this information, as I have never seen a black doctor on TV. But the look of kindness in his handsome face reassures me. I imagine my small white face pressed against his strong black chest. The secretary leaves and the doctor asks me a few questions. "Why do you think you're a homosexual?" "Because I like men," I tell him. "What do you want to do with them?" "I don't know—just be with them," I offer, searching for the correct answers, "and give them blow jobs." "Where did you learn that word?" "In *Everything You Always Wanted to Know About Sex* by David Rueben, M.D.," I reply. Dr. Casey seems satisfied with my answers and then rises from behind his desk. "I'd like to help you," he says. "But you understand I can't possibly treat you without the permission of your mother."

[*Horror music.*]

He hands me the phone. "I'm afraid you'll have to call her and tell her where you are."

[*Sound: air raid sirens.*]

I dial my mother's phone number at work, unable to look him in the eyes. "Hello Mom?" "I'm at a doctor's office." "No, nothing's wrong."

I hand the phone to Dr. Casey. "I think you should come down and pick your son up," he says. "313 Franklin Street." He hangs up the phone. "I'm sorry," he says. I look into Dr. Casey's eyes. [*Pause*] "I… You… Nigger!"

[*Sound: a horror movie scream.*]

[*The BOY puts his hands over his ears. A beat.*]

My mother collects me at Dr. Casey's office and she tells him: "What he's lacking is a male role model." Dr. Casey agrees and offers to treat me, but my mother nervously replies that, "There is a Dr. Kaplan in town, who I think would be a more appropriate choice for us." We walk briskly to the car. We sit in front of Dr. Casey's office in silence. My mother lights a cigarette.

"Why didn't you tell me about this…problem?" "There is no problem, l feel better already." "Really, I think it's just a passing phase you're going through." "Yes, I feel it passing already as we speak." "What would you like for dinner?" "Can we go to McDonald's?" "Yes, I think that's a wonderful idea."

And that's the last we talk about it. Years pass.

I look at myself in the mirror as I prepare to meet my mother in New Jersey. After thirty years I must admit my boyish good looks and full head of hair have not diminished. I look remarkably like my dead father. An irony I am not unaware of.

I take the bus from New York City to my mother's small apartment. We see each other often, my mother and myself. We share an easy intimacy. As easy as either of us is capable. We even talk about my boyfriends.

Tonight my mother's taking me to dinner at McDonald's. Close and within walking distance, it is most convenient now that she doesn't drive anymore.

[*Muzak.*]

I haven't been to a McDonald's in years, but it's the same as I remember it. It's different; but it hasn't really changed. It's like Cher.

My mother and I eat Big Macs and talk about current events. My mother is ecstatic about the passing of the "Gay Marriage Bill" in Vermont. She looks forward to the day I settle down with someone. She wants me to have the kind of love she had with my father. To not be lonely.

"Are you lonely?" I ask her. "No, no. I have so many friends," she says. "Why didn't you ever remarry?" "After your father, there was nobody else for me. You know that." "Do you miss him?" she asks. "Yes," I answer. "I miss him very much."

She delicately chews on a French fry. "I miss him too." She takes a gulp of Diet Sprite. McDonald's seems to be making her nostalgic.

"But I wish I had done a better job, with you...after...," she says. "You know, I still feel bad about when you went to see that psychiatrist, what was his name?" "Dr. Casey," I answer. "I should never have made him call me." "Oh, Ma," I say, "You're confused. He made ME call YOU. He was a bad psychiatrist. He betrayed my trust."

And then it all comes out:

"No." "I never told you this, but I opened that letter you got from Dr. Casey, you know saying he would see you. I made him have you call me from his office. I told him I'd sue him if he didn't. I was so desperate to know why you contacted him. I didn't know what else to do."

[*Sound: sirens.*]

And suddenly it feels like I am falling. As if the room around me is falling away:

"Darling." "I'm sorry." "Please forgive me." "I love you."

"It's O.K.," I say. I stare at my hot apple pie. "You did the best you could." I start to form the words I love you. "I…love…" Inside myself I hear the roar of wind and the sound of combustion.

"I love you, Ma. I forgive you. I love you. Of course, I love you."

[*Music: "Heatwave" bumps up.*]

…And suddenly the flames of love engulf me. I see the plastic chairs begin to melt. The tables bursting into fire. I smell the stench of burning flesh, and as McDonald's is consumed I scream for help…

…Then all at once my dead father appears and takes my hand. He pulls my mother to her feet. With him are *his* mother Rebecca, his sister Rachel, his first wife Betsy, and their son Wolf. Dr. Casey joins us—and David Rueben, M.D.—and as the plastic burns around us, we all begin to dance together.

We form a huge conga line and we dance. We dance and we dance and we dance, through the flames.

[*Lights fade.*]

• • •

Kitty the Waitress

Christopher Durang

Christopher Durang

Christopher Durang's plays include *A History of the American Film* (Tony nomination, Best Book of a Musical), *The Actor's Nightmare, Sister Mary Ignatius Explains It All for You* (Obie Award, Off-Broadway run 1981–83), *Beyond Therapy* (on Broadway in 1982, with Dianne Wiest and John Lithgow), *Baby with the Bathwater* (Playwrights Horizons, 1983), *The Marriage of Bette and Boo* (Public Theater, 1985; Obie Award, Dramatists Guild Hull Warriner Award), *Laughing Wild* (Playwrights Horizons, 1987) and *Durang Durang* (an evening of six plays at Manhattan Theatre Club, 1994, including the Tennessee Williams parody *For Whom the Southern Belle Tolls*). In 1996, he was commissioned by the Rodgers and Hammerstein Foundation to write a new book for the popular musical *Babes in Arms*. *Sex and Longing* was commissioned by Lincoln Center Theater and was presented on Broadway in fall 1996 starring Sigourney Weaver. *The Idiots Karamazov*, a full-length play with music written with Albert Innaurato, was revived at the American Repertory Theatre. His play *Betty's Summer Vacation* (Drama Desk Award nomination) had its world premiere at Playwrights Horizons in February 1999 to great critical acclaim and sold-out houses and was extended three times. It was the recipient of four Obie Awards, for distinguished playwriting, directing, acting, and set design. His new musical (with music by Peter Melnick), *Adrift in Macao*, premiered at New York Stage and Film in the summer of 2002.

Mrs. Bob Cratchit's Wild Christmas Binge was commissioned by Pittsburgh's City Theater and had its world premiere in November 2002. In the early '80s, he and Sigourney Weaver co-wrote and performed in their acclaimed Brecht-Weill parody, *Das Lusitania Songspiel*, and were both nominated for Drama Desk Awards for Best Performer in a Musical. In 1993, he sang and tried to dance in the five-person Off-Broadway Sondheim revue, *Putting It Together*, with Julie Andrews at Manhattan Theatre Club. And he played a singing Congressman in *Call Me Madam* with Tyne Daly as part of New York City Center's *Encores!* series.

Since 1994 he has been co-chair with Marsha Norman of the Playwriting Program at the Juilliard School in Manhattan. He is a member of the Dramatists Guild Council.

· · · **production history** · · ·

Kitty the Waitress was first presented in an evening called *Nine Lives* at the Juilliard School, Drama Division, in New York City, on February 21 and 22, 1997. The evening was a series of nine plays, all about the lives of a cat. The other eight plays were by Hilary Bell, Ron Fitzgerald, Daniel Goldfarb, Jessica Goldberg, Bob Kerr, David Lindsay-Abaire, Marsha Norman, and Alexandra Tolk. The evening was directed by Elizabeth Gottlieb; the program coordinator was Richard Feldman; and production stage manager was Scott Rollison. The cast for *Kitty the Waitress* was:

HOSTESS   Claire Lautier
MR. O'BRIEN   Peter Jacobson
KITTY   Greg McFadden*
WAITER   Erin Gann
VERONIQUE   Pamela Nyberg
VETERINARIAN   Dave Case

· · · **production note** · · ·

*The part of KITTY is meant to be played by a woman. For the purpose of the *Nine Lives* evening, we chose to have the cat in each play played by the same actor, necessitating having a male actor play the waitress in my play and a fading female cat star in Bob Kerr's play. The other seven plays all had a male cat in them. Greg McFadden did a terrific job as the waitress in my play; but especially if you present the play on its own, I prefer that KITTY be played by a woman.

Subsequent to this production, *Kitty the Waitress* was included in the evening *Mix and Match Durang*, presented by Birnam Wood, Tracey Becker, and Nellie Bellflower, producers, at the John Drew Theatre, in East Hampton, New York, on June 27 and 28, 1997. The evening was directed by Elizabeth Gottlieb. The cast was as follows:

HOSTESS   Claire Lautier
MR. O'BRIEN   Peter Jacobson
KITTY   Penny Balfour
WAITER   Michael Ian Black
VERONIQUE   Jennifer Van Dyck
VETERINARIAN   Jonathan Walker

characters

THE HOSTESS, gracious and French

MR. O'BRIEN, American

KITTY, the waitress, seductive, and French

THE WAITER

VERONIQUE, another waitress

THE VETERINARIAN

. . .

[*Scene: A restaurant on a tropical island. An American man,* MR. O'BRIEN, *enters. He is in his early 30s to early 40s. He is greeted by a friendly, effusive French woman, who is* THE HOSTESS *and owner of the restaurant. She has a French accent.*]

HOSTESS Oh, Monsieur Au Briand, comment ca va?

O'BRIEN Fine, merci.

HOSTESS Did you 'ave a lovely day at the beach?

O'BRIEN Yeah, yeah. My ex-wife won total custody of our kid today. I get to see him for two hours when he turns 12, and then again when he's 16.

HOSTESS Oh, Monsieur, quelle dommage. Well, forget your troubles here on our beautiful island, and we at this restaurant will do all we can to soothe you.

O'BRIEN Thank you. I'm feeling kind of gloomy.

HOSTESS Oh, Monsieur. We lighten your troubles for you. Forget your wife, forget your child. You are in tropical paradise.

O'BRIEN Yes, thank you. I am in paradise, right.

HOSTESS   Your usual table, Monsieur.

O'BRIEN   Yeah, I mean, oui.

HOSTESS   Oui, Monsieur.

[*Guides him to his table; motions for him to sit:*]

Si vous plait.

[O'BRIEN *sits.*]

Veronique will be your waitress tonight, Monsieur. Bon apetite.

O'BRIEN   Thank you.

[THE HOSTESS *goes away. After a moment,* KITTY *enters. She is very seductive, seductively dressed. She walks over to* O'BRIEN's *table, and then stands in front of him. Whenever she stands, she has a pronounced curve to her posture; she pushes her lower body forward. It seems seductive, but also a little weird. It should seem odd and explicit, but not like a contortion; her stance should be comfortable for her. It's just her pelvis that pushes forward.* KITTY *is extremely flirtatious in her manner as well, in a very generalized way. She speaks in a French accent.*]

KITTY   Bonjour, Monsieur. My name is Kitty, I will be waitress ce soir.

O'BRIEN   I thought my waitress' name was Veronique.

KITTY   No, Monsieur. My name is Kitty. Je m'appelle Kitty, le chat d'amour.

O'BRIEN   Well, okay. Hiya, Kitty.

KITTY   Bonjour, Monsieur.

[*She moves her lower body around in a circle, seductively.*]

Would you like something to drink, Monsieur?

O'BRIEN   [*Responding to her flirtatiousness.*] A bottle of water. A bottle of wine. A hunk of cheese. Et vous, Mademoiselle.

KITTY   [*Laughs seductively.*] Et moi? Oh, no, Monsieur. Non, non, non. Kitty is not on ze menu.

O'BRIEN   Well, why are you standing that way then? Pull your private parts in.

[KITTY *stands straight for a moment, pulling in her lower body so that her pelvis does not thrust forward. However, this posture is difficult to her. The "pelvis out" one is the one that feels natural to her. However, for now, she does her best to stand straight.*]

KITTY   Would you like to 'ear the specials, Monsieur?

O'BRIEN   Okay. Shoot.

KITTY   Tonight we 'ave filet of red snapper avec un sauce of artichokes et sardine. We 'ave Mahi Mahi avec un sauce de Mieu Mieu, in honor of ze French actress Mieu Mieu. The fish is flown by aeroplane from ze island of Maui.

O'BRIEN   Mahi Mahi from Maui avec Mieu Mieu sauce.

KITTY   Oui, Monsieur.

[*Unable to stand straight anymore, she reverts to her old posture, and lets her lower body thrust out again with relief; she explains seductively.*]

I 'ave ze bad posture, Monsieur.

O'BRIEN   No, it's charming in its way. It's just I haven't had a woman in over a year. And your posture upsets me.

KITTY   [*Flirting.*] I do not know what you mean, Monsieur.

[*Back to the specials.*]

We 'ave mussels meuniere, we 'ave salade du crab, we 'ave tuna grille avec Gerard Depardieu sauce; et finalement, we 'ave le specialité de la maison, le filet du soleil avec roast mouse et parakeet gratineé. Meow, meow, c'est une grande delicaceé.

[*Shakes her lower body at him in ecstasy.*]

O'BRIEN   Kitty, please. I told you, I haven't had a woman in a year.

KITTY   Oui? Quelle dommage, Monsieur. Et what would you like from ze menu zis evening?

O'BRIEN   Well, the specials sound interesting, especially that Maui Maui fish served with Muck Muck sauce. But, what I would like is a good old American hamburger, cooked rare, with French fries and cole slaw. I hope you don't think badly of me by my order.

KITTY   Pas du tout, Monsieur. Kitty does not judge. Kitty loves all choices, she sees no difference between any of zem. But let me tell ze kitchen of your wishes.

[*Screams out, a bit vulgar.*]

Hey, Mario! Gimme a Number 42, with grease and slaw, bloody!

[*Back to* O'BRIEN; *flirtatious and French again.*]

Anything else, Monsieur, you wish from Kitty?

[*She waves her lower body at him again.*]

O'BRIEN   Not right now. Thank you very much.

KITTY   Oui, Monsieur.

[KITTY *walks away seductively, exits. A young* WAITER, *cute, comes on, holding a basket of bread. He comes over to* O'BRIEN *and, like* KITTY, *sticks out his lower body and waves it at him.*]

WAITER [*Waving his lower body seductively; French accent.*] Would you like a basket of bread, Monsieur?

O'BRIEN What?

WAITER Basket, Monsieur?

[*Waves his lower body with energy.*]

O'BRIEN No, go away. I'm not interested.

[WAITER *puts bread on table, walks away, annoyed or disappointed in the response; exits.*]

[*To himself.*] What island am I on exactly, I wonder?

[KITTY *appears right, across the stage from* O'BRIEN. *She holds a bottle of wine and a glass.*]

KITTY I am bringing you ze wine, Monsieur.

[KITTY *raises the bottle and the glass into the air.* THE WAITER *comes back, next to* KITTY, *and begins to play the bongo drums.* KITTY *begins to dance towards* O'BRIEN *with the wine, but with very slow, samba-like movements, always leading with her lower body. It is a seductive, strange dance she is doing. Her dance does take her toward the table, but it will take a very, very long time for her to actually get to* O'BRIEN *if she keeps going at this slow, seductive, rhythmic speed.* KITTY *smiles delightedly while she does this dance, and keeps moving her hips at that pelvic area of hers.*]

O'BRIEN [*Stares for a while; eventually becomes impatient.*] Faster, faster! I haven't got all day.

[*The bongo rhythm goes much faster, and* KITTY *speeds up her dance movements and gets to his table much faster. The dance, sped up this way, looks much less sexy and much more peculiar, silly, an odd and unnecessary way to cross a room.* KITTY *arrives at the table.* THE WAITER *finishes the bongos with a definitive thump, and exits.*]

KITTY   Sometimes it takes a very long time to get across ze room.

O'BRIEN   Ah, yes. Does it?

[KITTY *puts the wine glass on the table, and holds up the wine bottle.*]

KITTY   Your wine, Monsieur.

> [KITTY *tries to pour the wine into the glass. However, the bottle is corked and nothing comes out of the bottle.*]

It ees not coming out, Monsieur.

O'BRIEN   Well, do you have a corkscrew?

KITTY   [*Blushingly flirtatious.*] Oh, Monsieur…a cork…screw??? Oh, Monsieur, you make Kitty blush avec your obscenities.

> [*Laughing like a school child.*]

Screw, screw? Oh, my, I am beside myself!

O'BRIEN   [*Sort of annoyed.*] Do you have a corkscrew to open the wine?

KITTY   [*Thinks; not flirtatious.*] No, I don't.

O'BRIEN   Well, take it away then.

KITTY   [*Calls offstage for* WAITER.] Gaston!

[THE WAITER *comes back and plays bongos again, so that* KITTY *can dance off with the wine. She dances away quickly this time. She and* THE WAITER *exit right. Another waitress,* VERONIQUE, *enters from left. She goes up to* O'BRIEN's *table.*]

VERONIQUE   [*Speaks with an over-the-top Cockney accent.*] 'Allo there, guv'nor! I'm your waitress, Veronique. 'Ow would you like a nice plate of beef and Yorkshire pudding, eh, ducks? Or a lovely cheese and tomato sandwich. Or a lovely shepherd's pie?

O'BRIEN   I'm sorry, your name is Veronique?

VERONIQUE   That's me name. I live in a flat with me mom, underneath the loo at Victoria Station. I come 'ere in the tube, and in the mornings I eat digestive biscuits.

O'BRIEN   I see. Kitty was waiting on me before.

VERONIQUE   We don't 'ave no Kitty 'ere, sir.

O'BRIEN   But she was just here. She did a dance to the bongo drums.

VERONIQUE   Bongo drums. Blimey, sir…your imagination is runnin' away with you.

O'BRIEN   She was just here. She walks funny.

VERONIQUE   Uh huh. Whatever you say, guv.

O'BRIEN   Never mind. Do you have a corkscrew?

VERONIQUE   What for?

O'BRIEN   For a bottle of wine. Oh, that's right, she took the wine away.

VERONIQUE   We don't serve wine 'ere, sir. 'Ow about a lovely lager, or a bit o'ale, or a nice cup a' tea served with a delicious bit of digestive biscuit.

O'BRIEN   Never mind. I'll wait for Kitty.

VERONIQUE   You'll wait a long time then, guv'nor.

[*Exits left.*]

O'BRIEN   [*Wanting* KITTY; *calling toward right, where she had exited.*] Oh, waitress! Oh, waitress!

[VERONIQUE *comes back on.*]

VERONIQUE   Yes?

O'BRIEN   No, I wanted Kitty.

VERONIQUE   [*Threatening a punishment.*] Do you want me to bring you your check?

O'BRIEN   Well, I haven't even eaten yet.

VERONIQUE   Then don't go on about Kitty please. Now you eat your bread and water, and if you're well be'aved, maybe Matron will reinstate your privileges.

O'BRIEN   What? Matron? Privileges? Am I in a play by Pirandello?

VERONIQUE   I'm sure I don't know, sir. [*Exits.*]

O'BRIEN   [*Calling, a bit softer.*] Kitty. Oh, Kitty.

[VERONIQUE *is back in, in a flash.*]

VERONIQUE   What did you say?

O'BRIEN   Nothing. I said absolutely nothing.

VERONIQUE   All right, then. [*Exits.*]

O'BRIEN   [*Waits a few seconds; then calls plaintively:*] Kitty…oh, Kitty…Here, Kitty, here, Kitty…I miss you. Oh, Kitty…

[VERONIQUE *comes back on, leading the* HOSTESS *and pointing to* O'BRIEN, *indicating there is some issue.* VERONIQUE *exits.*]

HOSTESS   Monsieur Au Briand, my apologies. Veronique has told me that the kitty was bothering you, I am so sorry.

O'BRIEN   What? No, no one was bothering me.

HOSTESS   I 'ave taken care that the kitty will bother you no more. We 'ave called up ze veterinarian, and 'e will put kitty to sleep momentarily.

O'BRIEN Put her to sleep? I don't know what you mean.

HOSTESS Please, do not feel bad. Many other guests have objected to the cat before…she rubs against the legs, they are allergic, she makes them sneeze. She make the bus boys play the bongos. She has been warned; it is only right she be put to death.

O'BRIEN Good God, where is the vet? I must stop this.

HOSTESS But your dinner, Monsieur….

O'BRIEN I don't want her death on my conscience. My ex-wife can't be right about me. I don't destroy all women I meet, do I?

HOSTESS I am sure I don't know, Monsieur.

O'BRIEN The address of the veterinarian…quickly, quickly!

HOSTESS Soixante-cinq, rue du chat du mort.

O'BRIEN Oh, God.

[O'BRIEN *runs off. Lights change, and we are in another part of the stage.* THE VET, *in a white coat, is standing over* KITTY, *who is in a fur coat (maybe) and lying on a cot.* THE VET *has just finished giving* KITTY *a shot from a hypodermic.*]

VETERINARIAN Bon nuit, Kitty.

O'BRIEN Wait, wait…don't give her a shot. She was my waitress. I loved her.

VETERINARIAN Too late. Ze kitty kat is on her way. Au revoir, kitty kat.

[*Exits.* O'BRIEN *kneels by* KITTY's *side.*]

O'BRIEN Kitty, Kitty, I'm here, don't die.

KITTY Good-bye, Monsieur. You did not love Kitty, and so the doctor, he gave me a shot. It ees time to leave. I 'ave danced enough.

O'BRIEN Oh, Kitty, no. I realize now. You're my reason for living.

KITTY Oh, Monsieur, do not try to cheer up a dying kitty. I am past it. I 'ave 'ad a full life. I 'ave lapped ze milk. I 'ave arched ze back. I 'ave eaten ze mouse, I 'ave chased ze parakeet. It ees time for Kitty to move on.

O'BRIEN No, I have nothing.

KITTY We 'ave Paris, Monsieur.

O'BRIEN We do? I don't remember anything about Paris.

KITTY Well, zen we 'ave nothing, Monsieur. Oh, the sodium pentathol is working. Au revoir, au revoir, I am leaving…life number…5, it is ending. Oh God, 4 more to go. So many disappointments, so many ze twists and ze turns. How difficile is la vie du chat. Oh…oh…c'est finie.

[KITTY *dies.* O'BRIEN *moans in sorrow and bows his head.* THE VET *comes in and gives* O'BRIEN *a hypodermic shot of something.* O'BRIEN *cries out in pain and looks surprised.*]

O'BRIEN Ow! What are you doing?

VETERINARIAN I am sorry, Monsieur. My mind, it wandered. I did not mean to give you a shot. But it is too late. Good-bye.

[O'BRIEN *looks shocked, then falls over dead.* VET *shrugs, what can you do? Lights out.*]

• • •

···property list···

Basket of bread (**WAITER**)

Bottle of wine (**KITTY**)

Wine glass (**KITTY**)

Bongo drums (**WAITER**)

Hypodermic needle (**VETERINARIAN**)

··· author's note: afterword ···

Since fall of 1994, fellow playwright Marsha Norman and I have been chairing a Playwriting Program at the Juilliard School, Drama Division, in New York City. We team teach—that is, we run class literally together. (Marsha and I obviously have different writing styles, but personally we got on very well, and have discovered that our thoughts and opinions on plays and on writing have much in common.) It is a one-year program, with a possible additional year residency fellowship for some of the students.

In 1996–97, we had seven students; and it was their idea to present an evening of short plays at Juilliard. Since with Marsha and me, that meant a total of nine writers, someone (or some combination of Alex Tolk, Hilary Bell, and Marsha) came up with the idea of writing plays about the nine lives of a cat. There were no rules, except we should let a person play the cat and we should limit the length to about nine minutes or so. We otherwise did no planning to coordinate, and all wrote what we wrote.

My play was inspired by an actual waitress I encountered on the island of St. Barths in the Caribbean, who over several days kept flirting with a friend of mine. She had this very seductive posture (not good for curvatures of the spine, I'm sure), where she tended to lean backwards slightly, in a relaxed stance, thus sort of "leading" with her lower body.

In terms of capturing this stance for the play, it's important that the stance be exaggerated, but not acrobatic, not like a gymnast about to flip over backwards. It is seductive, but it is also more or less comfortable for the actress, it just absolutely puts her pelvic area forward.

A few other tidbits of advice.

The accents are important. The actresses playing the Hostess and Kitty should be very comfortable with French accents and French pronunciations. Not only are there many French words and phrases in their dialogue, but there are also many English words they say that should nonetheless be said with French emphases (such as "restaurant," "Crab" with an *ah* sound, "parakeet"). I think it would be wise not to cast anyone who wasn't already knowledgeable about French pronunciation; but if you do, have someone handy to coach them well.

Similarly, Veronique's Cockney accent should also be a strong one (though I think that accent is easier to fake). Please, though, have the Cockney Veronique say her name with the right, proper French pronunciation. Don't make a joke that she says her name as Veron-ick; the joke is that she has a legitimate French name (Veron-neek), but is otherwise seeming smack dab in the middle of Piccadilly Circus.

When Kitty momentarily loses her French accent to call out Mr. O'Brien's hamburger order to the kitchen, don't get hung up wondering whether Kitty is only pretending to be French. She is French; I have her drop it for that moment alone for a joke—as if anytime you call to a kitchen it's in that loud, crass American way. (Or maybe it's his hamburger order that makes her make that transition.) But don't get stuck thinking it means more than it does.

Obviously, the play was written to fit into an evening of "cat" plays. (And thus Kitty's reference to "life number five" being over had more resonance when the play was fifth in the evening.) However, having just had the play done on its own this past summer, I think the play can also work on its own terms: a comedy about a ridiculously flirtatious waitress that then turns into a comic, bizarre fantasy where the waitress, it turns out, is also a cat.

I had a lot of fun writing this play; and the two times it's been done so far, it seems to go really well with the audience. If you choose to do it, I hope you have fun, too.

When I Was
a Little Girl
and My Mother
Didn't Want Me

Joyce Carol Oates

Joyce Carol Oates

Plays by Joyce Carol Oates have been performed at the Humana Festival of New Plays in Louisville; McCarter Theatre in Princeton; the Contemporary American Theater Festival in Shepherdstown, WV; the Circle Rep, American Place Theatre, and Ensemble Studio Theatre in New York; and in Paris, Stockholm, and Vienna. Her most frequently performed play is *I Stand Before You Naked* and her newest collection is *New Plays* (Ontario Review Press). She is the Roger S. Berlind Distinguished Professor in the Humanities at Princeton University and a member of the American Academy of the Arts and Letters. She is a recipient of the 1970 National Book Award and the 2003 Common Wealth Award for Distinguished Service in Literature.

*

[*Lights up. An elderly woman speaks. Her voice alternates between urgency and bemusement; emotion and reflection.*]

My father was killed and I never knew why.
Then, I was given away. By my mother.
I was so little…six months.
There were too many of us, nine of us, my mother gave me away.

When I was old enough to know…I cried a lot.
My father was killed and I never knew why.
No one would tell me.
Now there's no one I can ask.
"Why? Why?"
It happened in a fight, in a tavern, he was only forty-four
 years old.
My father I never Knew. Forty-four! Now, he could be my son.

I wasn't always an…old woman. Eighty-one.
I was a girl for so long. I was a little girl for so long.
I was six months old when my father died.
And there were too many of us to feed, and my mother…gave
 me away.

There were nine children. I was the baby.
I was born late, I was the baby.
My mother gave me to her sister Lena who didn't have children.
 This was in 1918.
This was in the Black Rock section of Buffalo, the waterfront on
 the Niagara River.
Germans, Poles, Hungarians…immigrants.
We were Hungarians. We were called "Hunkies."
I don't know why people hated us…

[WOMAN *pauses; decides not to explore this.*]

Uncle John and Aunt Lena were my "parents."
We moved to a farm far away in the country.
And my real mother and my brothers and sisters moved to a farm
  a few miles away.
Uncle John and Aunt Lena were good to me.
I don't know if I loved them…I think I loved them. I think…
I think they loved me.
They wanted children but couldn't have them so it was right, I
  think, that my mother gave me to them…

[*Pause.*]

It was a, a good thing, it was a…necessary thing.
I would learn one day that it happened often.
In immigrant families in those days.
In poor immigrant families.

My father was killed and I never knew why.
They said he was a bad drinker, he got drunk and was always in
  fights.
The Hungarians were the worst, they said—the drinking, and the
  fighting.
They said he was so handsome, my father.
My mother Elizabeth was so pretty.
Curly hair like mine.
They said he had a temper "like the devil."
In the tavern there was a fight, and he died.
A man took up a poker and beat my father to death.
I never knew why, I never knew who it had been.
Yet this was how my life was decided.

There is the moment of conception—you don't know.
There is the moment of birth—you don't know.
There is the moment your life is decided—you don't know.
Yet you say, "This is my life."

You say, "This is me."

[WOMAN *regards herself in wonder like a stroke victim regaining some of her awareness.*]

> When I was a little girl and my mother didn't want me I hid
>   away to cry.
> I felt so bad and I felt so ashamed.
> When I was old enough I would walk to the other farm.
> There was a bridge over the Tonawanda Creek a few miles away.
> They didn't really want to see me I guess.
> My name was Carolina, but they didn't call me that.
> I don't remember if there was a name they called me.
> They weren't very nice to me I guess.
> They didn't want me, I guess I was a reminder of…something.
>
> Elizabeth, my mother, never learned English.
> She spoke Hungarian all her life.
> She never learned to read. She never learned to drive a car.
> My Aunt Lena never learned to drive, so the sisters didn't see
>   much of each other.
> They lived only a few miles apart, and were the only sisters of
>   their family in America, but they didn't see much of each other.
> That was how women were in the old days.
> She was a short, plump woman.
> Curly brown hair like mine.
> People would say, "You look just like your momma!"
> Then they would be surprised, I'd start to cry.
> My mother scolded me in Hungarian—
> "Go away, go home where you belong. You have a home.
> Your home is not here."
>
> I loved my big brothers and sisters.
> There was Leslie, he was the oldest.

He took over when my father died.
There was Mary, I didn't get to know real well.
They were born in Budapest.
There was Steve, who'd been kicked and trampled by a horse.
 His brain was injured, he would never leave home.
There was Elsie who was my "big sister."
There was Frank who was my "big brother."
There was Johnny…and Edith…
There was George, I wasn't too close with George.
There was Joseph, I wasn't too close with.

[*Pause.*]

They are all dead now.
I loved them, but…
I am the only one remaining.
Sometimes I think: The soul is just a burning match!
It burns a while and then…
And then that's all.

It's a long time ago now, but I remember hiding away to cry.
When I was a little girl and my mother didn't want me.

• • •

Chad Curtiss— Lost Again: Episode 14: "Revelations"

Arthur Kopit

Arthur Kopit

Arthur Kopit's plays include *Oh Dad, Poor Dad, Mama's Hung You in the Closet and I'm Feelin' So Sad* (Vernon Rice Award, Outer Circle Award); *Indians* (Tony Nominee); *Wings* (Tony Nominee, Prix Italia for radio version of play); *End of the World with Symposium to Follow*; a new translation of Ibsen's *Ghosts; Road to Nirvana;* the book for the musical *Nine* (Tony Award for Best Musical 1982 and Best Revival of a Musical 2002); the book for the musical *Phantom*, based on Gaston Leroux's *The Phantom of the Opera* (music and lyrics by Maury Yeston); and, most recently, the book for *High Society*, a musical based on Philip Barry's *The Philadelphia Story*, with music by Cole Porter, which recently premiered on the West End. *Phantom*, written prior to the Lloyd Webber version, has played in theatres around the country, and has had long-running successful tours in Germany and Scandinavia. Also, various one-act plays, including *Chamber Music, The Day the Whores Came Out to Play Tennis, Conquest of Everest, The Questioning of Nick, The Hero, Success,* and *Good Help Is Hard to Find.*

Television films include the NBC mini-series *Hands of a Stranger;* the NBC mini-series of his *Phantom of the Opera*, the CBS mini-series *In a Child's Name*, and *Roswell.*

Recent projects include: *BecauseHeCan* (formerly entitled *Y2K*), which had its premiere as part of Actors Theatre of Louisville's annual Humana Festival and was presented in New York by Manhattan Theatre Club and recently at the McCarter Theatre (as well as productions in Germany and Scandinavia); an original musical, *Tom Swift and the Secrets of the Universe*, for which he is writing the book, and Maury Yeston the music and lyrics; and a new play, *Discovery of America*, based on the journals of the Spanish explorer, Cabeza de Vaca.

Mr. Kopit is the recipient of numerous awards, including: Shaw Traveling Fellowship, Harvard, 1959; Guggenheim Fellowship, 1967; Rockefeller grant, 1968; Award for Literature, American Institute of Arts and Letters, 1971; and an N.E.H. grant, 1974. He has also taught playwriting at the Yale School of Drama (from 1976–80), where he was a CBS Fellow; at Columbia University; at NYU; and, from 1981–94, at CCNY. He is a member of the Dramatists Guild, the Dramatists Guild Council, the Writers Guild of America, and PEN.

Mr. Kopit is married to the writer Leslie Garis. They live in New York City and have three children: Alex, Ben, and Kathleen.

characters

CHAD (as a young boy)

CHAD (20 years older)

CHAD'S BELOVED MOTHER

CHAD'S UNCLE BEN (a man of the cloth)

EVELYN EVANGELINE RUE (as a Mysterious Young Girl)

GENERAL ZARKO (a madman, bent on Chad's destruction)

ENGSINFLAGGNN (the "Shape Shifter from Hell")

EVELYN EVANGELINE RUE (grown up, but as mysterious as ever)

HAMMERHEAD (a mutant, in GENERAL ZARKO's employ)

K-3 (an albino spy, in GENERAL ZARKO's employ)

K-4 (K-3's albino twin, also in GENERAL ZARKO's employ; *played by same actor who plays Hatchet*)

A VOICE IN THE DARK

• • •

[*In the dark, a man's deeply sonorous voice begins to intone Canto I of Dante's "Inferno." Let us call him,* THE READER. *His voice is not one we've heard before.*]

THE READER

> Nel mezzo del cammin di nostra vita
> mi ritrovai per una selva oscura
> ché la diritta via era smarrita.

[*Now we hear music: something majestic and calm, like the second theme in Verdi's overture to* La Forza del Destino.]

[*And now the lights rise.*]

[*Corpses lie everywhere, many dismembered savagely, and rotted beyond recognition.*

Some of the bodies, perhaps to preserve their flesh for leaner times, hang down on hooks, like racks of beef.]

> Ahi quanto a dir qual era è cosa dura
> esta selva selvaggia e aspra e forte
> che nel pensier rinova la paura!
>
> Tant'è amara che poco è più morte;
> ma per trattar del ben ch'i' vi trovai,
> dirò de l'altre cose ch'i' v'ho scorte.
>
> Io non so ben ridir com'i' v'intrai,
> tant'era pien di sonno a quel punto
> che la verace via abbandonai.
> [*Beat.*]

[*Our* READER, *having come to the end of the first twelve lines of Canto I, begins again. For the remainder of this scene, he will never get past those twelve lines.*]

> Nel mezzo del cammin di nostra vita
> mi ritrovai per una selva oscura
> ché la diritta via … (etc.)

[*Now* OTHER READERS *join in.*]

SECOND READER

> Midway upon the journey of our life
> I found myself within a forest dark,
> For the straightforward pathway had been lost.
>
> Ah me! how hard a thing it is to say
> What was this forest savage, rough, and stern,
> Which in the very thought renews the fear.
>
> Midway upon the journey of our life
> I found myself within a forest dark,

For the straightforward pathway had been lost.
(etc.)

THIRD READER

Midway on our life's journey,
I found myself in dark woods,
The right path lost.

To tell about these woods is hard—
so tangled, rough, and savage—
that thinking of it now, I feel
The old fears stirring.
(etc.)

[*As* THE VOICES *fade, a familiar voice is heard.*]

VOICE IN THE DARK   Years have passed. General Zarko's forces have
been routed by infidels searching for the same sacred tablet that
by now *everyone* seems to be looking for.

[*Enter, the real* EVELYN EVANGELINE RUE, *bruised, filthy dirty, her sweet dress
in tatters, and so weak she can hardly walk.*]

Everyone who's still alive, that is.

[*Yet, like some young Mother Courage,* EVELYN *forges on, undaunted, a dusty, once-
elegant hatbox clutched in her right hand, a large sack held in her left.*]

The general's terrible doomsday machine—code-name "Iron
Chef"—which chopped off Chad's head just as he was about to
remember where the sacred tablet was hidden, has self-destructed.
A world of desolation lies everywhere. And now, Episode 14,
"Revelations."

[*Heaving a weary sigh,* EVELYN *sits and stares out glumly.*]

MUFFLED VOICE Dongivvup.

[*She opens the hat box cover and peers in.*]

EVELYN EVANGELINE RUE What?

CHAD'S VOICE [*From inside the hatbox!*] Don't give up.

EVELYN EVANGELINE RUE I'm not.

CHAD'S VOICE Well, it doesn't feel that way.

EVELYN EVANGELINE RUE What are you talking about?

CHAD'S VOICE I sense a defeatist attitude coming over you.

EVELYN EVANGELINE RUE Chad, let me tell you something. As far as I'm concerned, you are in no position to talk, 'cause you can't see what *I* see.

CHAD'S VOICE What's there to see—a few palm trees, a pretty beach?

EVELYN EVANGELINE RUE Chad, we are not in Florida.

CHAD'S VOICE You told me we were in Florida!

EVELYN EVANGELINE RUE I was lying.

CHAD'S VOICE *Lying?*

[*Evelyn opens the hatbox and peers in.*]

EVELYN EVANGELINE RUE Chad?

CHAD'S VOICE I'm not talking to you ever again!

EVELYN EVANGELINE RUE Chad, I'm sorry I lied. It's the only time in my life I ever have.

CHAD'S VOICE   (*Sudden hope.*) Is that true?

EVELYN EVANGELINE RUE   No. Oh Chad, what's to become of us? I've just lost my moral center, you've lost your body.

[*Enter, a* LARGE MUTANT SPIDER—*actually, not a spider at all, but* ENGSIN-FLAGGNN, *the shape-shifter from hell. Evelyn stares at it, disgusted.*]

CHAD'S VOICE   Well, I love you anyway.

EVELYN EVANGELINE RUE   [*Eyes on the spider, slowly making its way towards her.*] Thank you.

CHAD'S VOICE   When I find God's tablet and fulfill my destiny, do you think you'd maybe like to marry me?

EVELYN EVANGELINE RUE   [*Focused on the spider.*] Sure.

CHAD'S VOICE   Even if we don't find any more body parts for me?

EVELYN EVANGELINE RUE   [*Paying more attention to the spider than* CHAD.] We'll find more.

CHAD'S VOICE   What's the count so far?

[*That snaps her back, and she checks inside her sack.*]

EVELYN EVANGELINE RUE   Four arms, three legs (one of them missing a foot), five—no, sorry…

[*She digs around.*]

…six penises…

CHAD'S VOICE   We'll need something to attach them to.

EVELYN EVANGELINE RUE   *Them?*

CHAD'S VOICE   Why not?

EVELYN EVANGELINE RUE   You'll look funny with six penises.

CHAD'S VOICE   No funnier than I look now.

[*The spider stops a short distance away, hunkers down, and just watches them.*]

> But if it's at all possible, I'd rather have them as part of my groin than my head.

EVELYN EVANGELINE RUE   Wait! I think I see a groin!

> [*Leaving the hatbox hidden as best she can, she rushes off toward a mound of dead bodies, looking for a spare groin.*]

[*The moment her back is turned, the spider rushes, spiderlike, to the hatbox, grabs it with her beak, pincers, whatever, and waddles off with it, chortling as only mutant spiders can.*]

CHAD'S VOICE   [*As he's being carried away.*] Evelyn? …

> [*First signs of worry.*]

> Evelyn, is that you?

[*Exit,* ENGSINFLAGGNN *with hatbox. Meanwhile,* EVELYN *is tugging at something buried in the mound of bodies.*]

EVELYN EVANGELINE RUE   [*To the hatbox, not realizing it isn't there anymore.*] If this is what I think, you may not need those other six.

> [*She pulls… It gives!—the lower portion of man's multitattooed torso, which she has yanked out of its enclosure by a penis any horse would be proud of. Still holding it by its penis, she turns triumphantly. Which is when she realizes the hatbox and spider are gone.*]

> Shit!

[*To the heavens.*] Sorry!

[EVELYN, *still holding the penis, races off after the spider and Chad. In so doing, Evelyn practically runs into someone we cannot see—at least, not yet.*]

[*Offstage, to the unseen person.*]

Woops! Sorry!

[*The unseen person, a man, mutters some incomprehensible but clearly surly reply. We sense he's in great pain.*]

[TWO OTHER VOICES, *also men's, can be heard.*]

FIRST MAN   [*Offstage.*] Don't worry, we've got you!

SECOND MAN   [*Offstage, overlapping.*] If you could maybe just lift this leg a little bit *more…*

FIRST MAN   [*Offstage.*] …And this *arm…*

[*Enter, GENERAL ZARKO, looking shockingly terrible, and unable to walk on his own for reasons related to his new physical state: his legs have somehow been stretched to about three times their normal length, and flattened. His arms, as flat as his legs, have also been stretched.*]

[*Assisting him—by propping him up under the armpits and pretty much dragging him—are two albino soldiers, K-3 and K-4, the last two men he feels he can still trust.*]

GENERAL ZARKO   Hurry! Hurry! They can't be far behind! *Goddam tanks! Don't get me the first time, they want to try again!* My own men! It's enough to make you weep. How many tanks ran over me?

K-3   Ten.

GENERAL ZARKO Ten fucking tanks!

K-4 Plus one amphibious landing vehicle.

GENERAL ZARKO Twelve fucking tanks plus three amphibious landing vehicles run over me and am I deterred? No. But as a leader of men, I am finished.

K-4 You can always teach.

GENERAL ZARKO Yes, but what?

K-3 Moral philosophy?

GENERAL ZARKO Oooh. I like the sound of that.

[*A shot rings out.*]

K-4 We have to go now.

[*Another gunshot.*]

K-3 Sorry.

[*As gunshots continue to ring out, they prop him up against a pile of corpses, and exit by running a serpentine route.*]

GENERAL ZARKO Wait-a-minute! Where are you going? I said wait-a-minute. WAIT-A-MINUTE!

[*Suddenly he sees something that gives him hope.*]

Oh, thank you Lord. Nurse! NURSE!

[*Enter,* CHAD'S MOTHER, *still in her S/M outfit, but with a saucy nurse's uniform over it. Gunshots continue.*]

CHAD'S MOTHER [*Sweetness itself.*] Did someone cry for help?

GENERAL ZARKO   Yes! Over here! Quick! Before they kill me!

CHAD'S MOTHER   [*As she approaches—merrily.*] Well, we certainly wouldn't want that, would we?

GENERAL ZARKO   Oh my God! *Mrs. Curtiss!*

[*She pulls out a giant hypodermic.*]

CHAD'S MOTHER   This may hurt a bit.

[*She plunges it into his heart. He screams.*]

[*Blackout.*]

A VOICE IN THE DARK   Later that night, in a seemingly abandoned mine shaft at the edge of a supposedly extinct volcano (but in reality a cavern measureless to man), Engsinflaggnn, the shape-shifter from hell, forms an unholy alliance with the Reverend Ben.

[*Lights up on "The Reverend Ben's Chamber of Horrors." In the gloomy vault, along with the* REVEREND—*his hands still in baggies—and* ENGSINFLAGGNN, *still a spider, but now, due to her strange skills, able to stand upright, is* CHAD—*or rather,* CHAD's *head, which is set on a marble pedestal, and well-lit, the open hat-box sitting nearby.*]

UNCLE BEN   So! My favorite nephew!—Headstrong as usual.

ENGSINFLAGGNN   Show him the sacred disk.

UNCLE BEN   The sacred disk! Coming up!

ENGSINFLAGGNN   I love the sacred disk! It's so *beautiful!*

CHAD   How did you find it?

UNCLE BEN   Remember when you were trapped in Antarctica by the Boxer Gang?

CHAD   No.

ENGSINFLAGGNN   What about, trapped in Latvia by the Beadle Group?

CHAD   That I remember.

UNCLE BEN   That's when we found it.

ENGSINFLAGGNN   And I helped him find it!

[*To the* REVEREND.] Didn't I, didn't I?

UNCLE BEN   [*Annoyed—all she seems to want is credit.*] Yes!

[*The* REVEREND BEN *opens a hidden cabinet. Inside, the sacred red disk glows eerily.*]

CHAD   But *how?*

ENGSINFLAGGNN   It would take too long to explain.

UNCLE BEN   BOX!

ENGSINFLAGGNN   *Box!*

[ENGSINFLAGGNN, *using whatever part of her anatomy she can, brings an insulated box to* UNCLE BEN, *who, using insulated tongs, slides the disk out of the cabinet and into the box.*]

UNCLE BEN   And now, my young friend, you are going to tell me what the message says.

CHAD   Never! Those four words were meant for my eyes only. So *I* could decide whether they should be revealed to the *rest* of the world—which includes *you.*

UNCLE BEN   [*Shouts into the darkness.*] Bring in You-Know-Who!

ENGSINFLAGGNN   Yes! The "You-Know-Who!"

[*Enter* K-3, *in monk's robes, leading the still-disheveled* EVELYN *by a chain.*]

CHAD   Evelyn!

EVELYN EVANGELINE RUE   I've decided. I *will* marry you, Chad!

CHAD   Oh Evelyn! That makes me so happy!

[*Enter* K-4, *also in monk's robes, leading* CHAD'S MOTHER, *still in her combo bondage suit and nurse's outfit, by chains.*]

CHAD   Mother?

CHAD'S MOTHER   Imhereforyouson.

CHAD   [*To his uncle.*] What?

[K-4 *unzips her mouth.*]

CHAD'S MOTHER   I'm here for you, son.

UNCLE BEN   [*To* ENGSINFLAGGNN.] Now show him the sacred disk.

ENGSINFLAGGNN   *"The sacred disk!"*

[*Music swells.* ENGSINFLAGGNN *walks over to Chad and opens the box. An eerie red light glows on* CHAD's *face.*]

UNCLE BEN   Tell us what the message says.

CHAD   [*Eyes averted.*] No! No! You can't make me!

ENGSINFLAGGNN   LOOK, DAMN YOU! LOOK!

CHAD   Noooo!

[*Suddenly, a strangely cold light falls on* UNCLE BEN. *Without willing it, a remarkable transformation is coming over him. A new and terrible strength has seized him, which seems to startle him as much as it does us.*]

[*When* UNCLE BEN *next speaks to* CHAD, *it is in a voice of dreadful authority.* SATAN *has entered* UNCLE BEN'*s body!*]

UNCLE BEN   [*A true Mephistopheles.*] Funny, I would have thought your curiosity was *stronger* than this.

CHAD   [*Stunned by the malevolent transformation.*] Uncle Ben!

UNCLE BEN   Not anymore.

CHAD   But…you were a man of *God!*

UNCLE BEN/SATAN   [*Pulling off his baggies.*] And still am. At our core, we are *all* men of God.

[*Looking up—with fury.*] ARE WE NOT!?

[*Sound of thunder, as if in response.*] Now read!

CHAD   No! God has put His faith in me, and I will not betray His faith.

UNCLE BEN   [*To* CHAD.] So which of these two should I kill first?

CHAD   [*A cry to the heavens.*] LORD, HELP ME!

UNCLE BEN   Fine. Then I will choose.

CHAD   [*To himself, eyes shut, like a mantra.*] I will not betray His trust, I will not betray His trust, I will not betray…(etc.)

[*While* CHAD *chants,* UNCLE BEN *points at* CHAD'S MOTHER.]

CHAD'S MOTHER   *Chaaaad…*

[CHAD *looks just as thunder crashes, electricity flies, and* CHAD'S MOTHER *screams, mortally done in by some fiendish power in the tips of* UNCLE BEN's *satanic fingers.*]

CHAD [*Utter horror.*] Mother!

CHAD'S MOTHER [*Weakening fast.*] You made…the right…choice, …son.

[*And with that, she collapses, dead.* UNCLE BEN *turns his malevolent gaze upon* EVELYN.]

UNCLE BEN And now the girl…

CHAD No!

EVELYN EVANGELINE RUE I love you, Chad Curtiss.

CHAD And I love you, Evelyn Evangeline Rue.

EVELYN EVANGELINE RUE I will *always* love you, Chad Curtiss.

CHAD And I will always love you, Evelyn Evangeline Rue.

UNCLE BEN Is that it, then?

CHAD I will not betray His trust, I will not betray His trust, I will not—

[*Thunder! Flashes of demonic light! And* EVELYN EVANGELINE RUE *crumples to the ground.* CHAD, *overwhelmed with despair, looks up.*]

Lord! Help me to understand!

[*Heavenly music is heard.* CHAD's *prayers have been answered! He looks down at the sacred disk, hoping for words of comfort… But what he sees does not comfort him.*]

…Oh my God… This cannot be…

UNCLE BEN   What! WHAT!

ENGSINFLAGGNN   [*The beast's voice.*] TELL US! TELL US!

UNCLE BEN   … What does it say?

ENGSINFLAGGNN   What does it say?

CHAD   It says…

[*Incredulous.*] …"Good-bye and good luck."

UNCLE BEN   "*Good-bye and g*—…" That's not possible.

CHAD   It's what it says!

UNCLE BEN   But He would never…

CHAD   I AM TELLING YOU WHAT IT SAYS!

UNCLE BEN   "Good-bye and good *luck*?"

CHAD   "Good-bye and good luck."

ENGSINFLAGGNN   That's five words, not four.

UNCLE BEN   "Good-bye" counts as one.

ENGSINFLAGGNN   Oh my God…

UNCLE BEN   It just doesn't make any sense!

[*Looking up.*] I thought we had a good relationship! I thought we understood each other! I mean, who is there to oppose me now? THIS IS NOT FIGHTING FAIR!

[UNCLE BEN *wanders off, in shock.* ENGSINFLAGGNN, *just as shocked, follows after him, forlorn.*]

ENGSINFLAGGNN [*As she leaves.*] Does it *always* count as one?

UNCLE BEN   Always. *Always!*

[*They exit.* CHAD *looks up to the heavens, terrified.*]

CHAD   Mother…if you can hear me…*I am scared!*

[*Lights fade to black.*]

A VOICE IN THE DARK   Will Chad "get himself together?"…Will God reconsider His decision and return? *Or*…Will something *else* occur, altogether unexpected? Be here next time…and, if you're very good, perhaps you will find out.

[*He laughs. As the music fades, the words* "TO BE CONTINUED" *appear briefly in the dark.*]

. . .

Deaf Day

Leslie Ayvazian

Leslie Ayvazian

Leslie Ayvazian has written the following full-length plays: *Nine Armenians* (John Gassner Award for best new play 1996–97; Roger L. Stevens Award; second place, Susan Smith Blackburn Prize; published in *Women Playwrights: The Best Plays of 1996*); *Singer's Boy* (produced at the American Contemporary Theatre, San Francisco); *High Dive* (produced at the Long Wharf Theatre, Manhattan Class Company, and others); *Rosemary and I* (finalist, Susan Smith Blackburn Award; workshop at New York Stage and Film, produced at Passage Theatre, Trenton, NJ); *Lovely Day* (produced at City Theatre, Pittsburgh PA; The Play Company, NY). Her new play is *Behave Yourself* (workshop Cape Cod Theatre Project and Adirondack Theatre Festival, 2006). Her first play, *Footlights*, was written in 1980 (Vineyard Theatre, NYC). She was a co-writer of the collaboration *Mama Drama* (Ensemble Studio Theatre; Cleveland Playhouse).

Ms. Ayvazian's one-act plays include *Practice; Plan Day; Deaf Day; Twenty Four Years; Hi There, Mr. Machine; Rosemary and Elizabeth* (Heideman Award finalist, Actor's Theatre of Louisville). All were produced by Ensemble Studio Theatre. Most plays have been published by Dramatists Play Service or Samuel French.

Ms. Ayvazian collaborated with Richard Greenberg on a pilot for HBO, *Emma in Concert*. She has written six children's plays for first to sixth graders.

setting

The set for *Deaf Day* is very simple: a chair.

Maybe a footstool.

Perhaps some toys on the ground.

time

Early morning for first scene.

Early evening for second scene.

· · · **production note** · · ·

Deaf Day can be performed by a deaf actor or hearing actor, a woman or a man. The Sign Language must be authentic.

· · · **production history** · · ·

Deaf Day was produced by the Ensemble Studio Theatre (Curt Dempster, Artistic Director) at their Marathon '99, 22nd Annual Festival of New One-Act Plays, in New York City in May 1999. It was directed by Leslie Ayvazian; the set design was by Kris Stone; the costume design was by Amela Baksic; the lighting design was by Greg MacPherson; the sound design was by Beatrice Terry; and the production stage manager was Gretchen Knowlton. It was performed by Kaitlyn Kenney.

Deaf Day is dedicated to Kaitlyn Kenney.

· · ·

[*A deaf mother talking to a deaf child, who does not appear on stage. Spoken aloud in English and also in Sign Language.*]

Ok.
Ready?
Come on!
Sun's up, Day's here.
Let's go!
Rise and shine.

That means: "Get up and…be happy!"
Come on.
Don't ignore me.
Look at me! Yes!

We have to practice English.
Yes. Today is practice day.
Your teacher said.
So look at me. Look at me!

Put your hearing aids in. Yes!

Now!

Good.

Ok.
We're going to the playground.
No, not at Deaf School.
In the Park.
Yes, there will be hearing children there.
I don't know if there will be any deaf kids.
You can speak to the hearing children.
Yes, you can.
Sure, you can.

Remember the new boy on our Street? Roger?
Maybe we'll see new boy Roger and his Dog!
You can talk to them. Yes!
And to other kids too.

Yes, you can.
You stand in front of them.
Look directly in their faces.

If they look away, say:

[*No Sign.*] "Could you please repeat that?"

[*No Sign.*] "Could you please repeat that?"

[*With Sign.*]

Yes, you can!

Say:

[*No Sign.*] "I can't hear you because I'm deaf."

[*Continues aloud and with Sign.*]

Some will laugh.
Some won't laugh.
Talk to the ones who don't laugh.
Come on, honey.
Yes.
Put your shoes on.
Put your shoes on!
I'll put them on you!
Then sit down and put them on!
Sit down!
Now tie your shoes.
Good.
Ok.
Get up.
Get up!
Get up!

Look at me!
Don't turn your head away.
Come on.
Ok.
I'll wait…

[*She waits. She taps her foot.*]

Hi.
Yes, I'll stay in the park with you, of course.
I'll sit on the closest bench.
You can talk to me whenever you want.
People may watch you.
And some may think: "WOW! Look at this kid!
He knows two languages! How cool!"

Well, some will think, "WOW!"
Some might be stupid.
We will ignore the stupid ones.
Do we feel sorry for the stupid ones?
Nah.
We think they're stupid.
But, some people will see how wonderful you are.
And those people will want to talk to you.
So, watch their faces.
Read their lips.

If they walk away without telling you where they are going, don't
be mad.
Hearing people talk with their back to each other.
At those times, wave to me.
We will talk.
And then, we'll come home. Yes.
And you can be quiet for as long as you want to be quiet.
No voices. Quiet.
Quiet.
Ok.

You ready?
Hearing aids, turned on!
Eyes open!

Let's go!

No, we don't have to march.
We can walk slowly!
We can walk real slowly.
And we'll look at each other.
And we'll talk.
In Sign.

We'll talk.

I promise. [*Without Sign.*]

Good. [*Without Sign.*]

[*Lights shift. Lights come up. It is the same day: evening. She speaks aloud and with Sign.*]

Hey.
It's almost time for bed!
Yes, it is!
And you have sleepy eyes.
Yes, yes, yes, you do.
But first…
Look at me, honey.

[*Hits floor for his attention.*]

[*In just Sign.*] Look at me! Good.

[*Continues aloud and with Sign.*]

Let's practice English before we go to bed.
Practice Day is nearly finished.

Watch my face.
Come on, watch.

Let's talk about the Park.
No. No Roger! No dog. No.

But the seesaw! Yes!
That girl!
No, we don't know her name.
But you two were perfectly balanced!
You sat in the air at the same time.
That's very special.

But the slide. I know.
They pushed you down the slide.
They wanted you to go faster.
They said: "HEY! …HEY!"

They didn't know that you couldn't hear them.
So, they pushed.
They pushed hard. I know.

It surprised you.
And it hurt you. I know.

They pushed you because they were frustrated with you.

But I think you can understand.
Sure you can.
Think about your deaf friends at school
When you want their attention, sometimes you grab
them. Sometimes you hit them. Sure you do.
Because you want them to look at you.
And you get frustrated. Yes, you do!

So, next time, if the kids are waiting, you go fast!
Ok!
Go fast down that slide.
You kick butt!

Yes!

Then no one will push you.
And no one will laugh.
You need to be fast and quick, quick, quick.
Like a bunny.
Yes.
A fast bunny who kicks butt!
That's you!
Yes!
Right! Jackie Chan!

Ok.

[*Jumps up and does Jackie Chan stance.*]

Jackie Chan!

Auhhhhhh!

[*Does Tae Kwon-Do kick.*]

We are Jackie Chan!

[*Another move.*]

But we have sleepy eyes!

Yes.

[*Said in Korean, no Sign.*] *Cha-Ryut. Kyung-Net.*

[*Bows to him.*] *Tae Kwon-Do.*

[*Back to Sign and English.*] So get in bed, Jackie Chan!

And maybe, tomorrow we'll go to the Planetarium.

Or the Zoo?

Maybe the Park.
And you can get back in the saddle.

That means: When you ride a horse and fall off, you
need to get back on the horse right away. So you don't
feel scared.

Back in the saddle.
Back in the Park.
Back on the slide.

Ok?

Ok.

Now sleep, honey.
Sweet dreams.

[*She waves.*]

Sweet dreams.

[*She leaves "his room" and sits. She waits. Then she gets back up and goes
to his room. She sees he is still awake, but sleepy. She waves again. She
leaves and goes back to her chair. She waits. Then she goes again and checks
on him. He's asleep. She returns to her chair and sits. She breathes a sigh
of relief. Beat. She notices he has walked into the room. She speaks aloud
and in Sign.*]

What's up?

Tomorrow?

Stay home?

All day?

No voices?

Quiet?

I'm thinking.

[*She gets up and sits on the floor.*]

Ok.

Tomorrow.

Quiet.

I promise.

Yes.

[*In just Sign.*] Quiet. Quiet. I promise.

[*In Sign and aloud.*] Good night.

[*In just Sign.*] Good night.

[*She sits watching her son. Lights fade.*]

• • •

Sisters of the Winter Madrigal

Beth Henley

Beth Henley

Beth Henley was awarded the Pulitzer Prize in Drama and the New York Drama Critics Circle Award for Best American Play for her play *Crimes of the Heart*. *Crimes* ran on Broadway at the Golden Theatre. A second play, *The Wake of Jamey Foster*, ran on Broadway at the Eugene O'Neill Theatre. Off-Broadway productions include *The Miss Firecracker Contest*, *The Lucky Spot*, *The Debutante Ball*, *Abundance*, *Impossible Marriage*, and *Family Week*. Ms. Henley's work has been produced internationally and translated into over ten languages. Smith and Kraus recently published a two-volume collection of her plays. Her newest play *Ridiculous Fraud* was produced at McCarter Theatre and also ran at South Coast Repertory theatre.

Ms. Henley wrote the screenplay for the acclaimed film version of *Crimes of the Heart*, for which she was nominated for an Academy Award. The film was directed by Bruce Beresford and starred Diane Keaton, Jessica Lange, Sissy Spacek, and Sam Shepard. She also wrote the screenplay for *Miss Firecracker* starring Holly Hunter and Tim Robbins. She wrote the screenplay for *Nobody's Fool*, which starred Rosanna Arquette and Eric Roberts, and co-wrote David Byrne's *True Stories*. Her television credits include *Surviving Love*, a film for CBS and starring Ted Danson and Mary Steenburgen, as well as a teleplay for the PBS series *Trying Times*, directed by Jonathan Demme.

· · · **production history** · · ·

Sisters of the Winter Madrigal was produced by Rolling Pictures in association with Moving Arts (Julie Briggs and Lee Wochner, Artistic Directors) in 2001. It was directed by Frederick Bailey; the set design was by Victoria Profitt; the sound and music design were by Sean Murray; the costume design was by Atsuko Ohtani Bailey; and the stage managers were Donnetta Grays and Alma Carrasco. The cast was as follows:

CALAIH   Cerris Morgan-Moyer
STEPHAN   Kris Kamm
ALEXTON   Cris D'Annunzio
TARETTA   Naomi Chan
MARDIAN   Camilla Carr
APOTHECARY   Valeri Ross
HIGH LORD   Tim Woodward
LETTER WRITER   Darrell Kunitomi
BLACKSMITH   Rudy Young
2 GUARDS   Darrell Kunitomi, Rudy Young

· · · **property list** · · ·

Medallions
Stick (**CALAIH**)
Cream, mirror (**TARETTA**)
Gold fan, silk, earrings, purple rock, headdress (**ALEXTON**, **TARETTA**)
Money pouch (**ALEXTON**)
Cheese (**CALAIH**)
Silver hairbrush (**CALAIH**)
Bags of money (**TARETTA**)
Milk, glass (**CALAIH**)
Scroll (**MARDIAN**)
Potion, bandages, tub (**APOTHECARY**)
Satchel (**STEPHAN**)
Papers, pens, lettering sheet (**LETTER WRITER**)

Silver comb (**CALAIH**)

Perfume (**TARETTA**)

Sewing things, wedding dress (**CALAIH**)

Silver shears (**MARDIAN, CALAIH**)

Dried apricots (**HIGH LORD**)

Long red braid (**CALAIH**)

Ax (**BLACKSMITH**)

Bloody handkerchief with ear inside (**CALAIH**)

characters

CALAIH

STEPHAN

ALEXTON

TARETTA

MARDIAN

APOTHECARY

HIGH LORD

LETTER WRITER

BLACKSMITH

2 GUARDS

place and time

Long ago in a land far away.

···scene one···

[*At night in the early autumn by the stream and hillside.* CALAIH *stands onstage holding a think stick, waiting. She is small with a plain face but she has beautiful red hair that reaches almost to the ground.* STEPHAN, *a tall young man, enters. He tosses pebbles into the stream.* CALAIH *moves closer to* STEPHAN *and breaks the stick in two. He turns to see her.*]

STEPHAN   Oh, it is you.

[*They stare at each other.*]

You are a strange girl. And yet they say the High Lord sent you a silver brush and comb for your long red hair. They say he is in love with you. I would use the word enchanted or fascinated or even curious myself. For I feel it is an impossibility to love someone with whom you have never even spoken. Where is your cow?

CALAIH   Eating grass up on the hill.

STEPHAN   Oh, so you do talk indeed. You must excuse me but so often I see you walking with your cow and I offer greetings and you say nothing, or you will come into my father's shop only to stare in silence and eat cheese while I laugh and tell stories as I work. Oh, there are times when you will come and hold your torn boots in your arms and nod up and down at my father—but never will you speak or smile or nod with me. Why can you not be like your sister, she is gay with every man. Excuse me. I regret mentioning it. There is nothing to be concerned about, Calaih.

CALAIH   The reason I do not speak to you is that I become timid. Do you know I walk up the hill and down again stamping over the sharpest rocks and stones only so my boots will be in need of repair and I may go to the shoemaker's shop to see you telling stories and laughing. My cow and me, we come here every night and stand on the hill to watch you sitting by this stream looking at the stars.

STEPHAN You watch me here at night?

CALAIH [*Nods.*] And sometimes you throw rocks.

STEPHAN I did not know that—I thought at times you must be—

CALAIH What?

STEPHAN Haughty.

CALAIH Haughty?

STEPHAN [*Nods.*] Because—because of your long fine hair and the gifts the High Lord sent to you and your quietness—to me, and because of my fondness for you…I like to watch you eating cheese.

CALAIH Do you love me then?

STEPHAN Yes.

CALAIH Good.

[*She goes and kisses him.*]

STEPHAN I must go now…

CALAIH Why do you go then?

STEPHAN My love is too deep.

CALAIH Please, you must love me in this soft grass, under the night stars. For I have loved you so long, Stephan the Shoemaker's Son.

STEPHAN Oh, Calaih, Orphan of Joshua the Cow Herder. You will get sticks and berries in your soft hair.

CALAIH Please, hold me. Hold me. It is cool here tonight.

[*They hold each other in the grass as the lights fade.*]

···scene two···

[*The same autumn night in* TARETTA's *room above the tavern.* TARETTA *is an attractive, sensual woman with dark hair and violet eyes. She sits at her dressing table rubbing cream on her arms and hands. She is wearing a beautiful, seductive robe.* ALEXTON's *voice is heard from outside.*]

ALEXTON'S VOICE Taretta. It is I.

TARETTA [*Picking up mirror.*] Come in, Alexton.

[ALEXTON *enters. He looks like a goose. He stands at the entrance nervously, holding a box.*]

I will be ready in a minute. You may get undressed if you like.

ALEXTON Oh, very well.

[*He undresses throughout the following segments.*]

I am glad you picked me tonight. I needed your company. My wife is a dowdy woman. This evening she went outside and sat in the dirt and cried.

TARETTA Yes, she is a very dowdy woman. Why did you marry her?

ALEXTON My life is sick and sad, Taretta. Without the sweet favors you bestow on me, I would be dead.

TARETTA Tell me, do you think the High Lord would wish to lie with me? Do you think he would enjoy being ravished by Taretta, Woman of Flaming Nights? That is how Heilington describes me—the Woman of Flaming Nights.

ALEXTON Do not speak of Heilington. This is my time with you, Taretta. Do not speak of others. Let them sit downstairs listening to your cries and shrieks knowing I am with you. Let them sit there and drown their sorrows alone, as I have done so many nights.

TARETTA   Ah, poor Alexton.

ALEXTON   Do not take any others tonight, Taretta. Let me be the only one.

TARETTA   If you can satisfy me, I will not. Now—shall I take off my robe?

[*He nods. She removes robe and stands before him in seductive undergarments.*]

ALEXTON   Here are the gifts I bring you. One gold fan. A piece of silk brought from my store. Two jeweled earbobs. A purple rock.

TARETTA   What is this? A rock? What do I want with a rock, Alexton?

ALEXTON   It is a purple rock. I found it by the stream. The purple is like that purple in your eyes, my dearest Taretta.

TARETTA   I have no use for a rock.

[*He takes it back.*]

ALEXTON   Here is something you will like.

[*He presents a headdress.*]

TARETTA   Lovely, very lovely. It will look well with my autumn gown. But I have see this somewhere before… I have seen it before indeed. This is your wife's headdress. She wore it only last week at the autumn festival with a very unsuitable gown. She will recognize this if I wear it.

TARETTA   I do not care. It suits you—not her.

TARETTA   Yes, but she will beat your children and your dog with a stick.

ALEXTON   And I will beat her with a limb off of the cypress tree. Wear it, I beg you…wear it alone with nothing and this gold is yours.

[*He holds up money pouch. She places on the headdress.*]

I will leave my dog with my brother. I do not want to have him beaten again.

· · · scene three · · ·

[*Early the next morning at the two sisters' cottage. CALAIH sits at the table, brushing sticks and grass and berries out of her hair and eating cheese. TARETTA enters, with a box of gifts and bags of money.*]

TARETTA   Good morning, sister.

CALAIH   Good morning.

TARETTA   Where is your cow?

CALAIH   Outside. He is lying in the sun.

TARETTA   I had quite an evening last night.

[*Dropping box and bags on the table.*]

Look at what Alexton has given me. There is a gold fan in there, silk from his shop, jeweled earbobs, and even his wife's autumn headdress. Here are the gold and coins I have gotten. This much from just Alexton alone; the rest is from all the others.

CALAIH   [*Touching the piece of silk.*] That is nice.

TARETTA   [*She begins counting money.*] Soon I will be leaving this hovel. I will get me a beautiful home near all the shops around the square. I have those debts left to pay on those new jewels and gowns, then I will be gone. Would you pour me some milk? My arm is aching.

CALAIH [*Pouring milk.*] Here.

TARETTA [*Drinking milk.*] You know, you are not so plain, Calaih. The High Lord even sent you that silver brush and comb. There is no reason for you to be poor. That is fifty there. But perhaps your appetites are not as developed as mine. I who can satisfy any man in any way. That makes seventy-five. But I will tell you a secret: Though these men are thoroughly nourished through my skills and charms. Ninety. There remains within me a deep craving. Do you understand that? As if one could pour hot gold into me for an eternity. And it would not be enough. A hundred there. But you do not understand. Though the High Lord sends you gifts, you could not meet his needs as I could. Ah, that makes one hundred and six. What a night.

[*She begins raking money into her purse.*]

CALAIH I am in love with Stephan the Shoemaker's Son, Taretta. This morning he walked me home with my cow, and he talked to us and petted my cow. He said, "This is a very fine cow you have." Then he said my name, "Calaih." Like that he said it, "Calaih."

TARETTA Stephan the Shoemaker's son. That strange boy? The one who always has a joke for you?

[CALAIH *nods.*]

I have always thought him a noodle. He will never be a rich man. But if you love him—if you love this noodle—

CALAIH You need not mock Stephan. He is dear to me and of greater worth than any of the baggage you have had.

TARETTA You speak in jealousy, Little Calf.

[MARDIAN, *an older woman with purple lips, enters. There are two guards behind her.*]

MARDIAN   Good morning. I am Mardian, Social Messenger to the High Lord. May I come in?

TARETTA   Yes. Come in.

MARDIAN   So you are Calaih, Orphan of Joshua the Cow Herder. Your hair is as lovely as they say. May I touch it?

[*She feels* CALAIH's *hair.*]

Now here is the proclamation I am to read to you. "Notice to all the Subjects. The High Lord proclaims he shall take Calaih, Orphan of Joshua the Cow Herder, as his Wife and High Lady. The ceremony is to take place on the last night of late winter. Only the bride and Special Attendants to the High Lord are to be allowed at the ceremony. However, there will be a public celebration the following morning on the first day of spring."

[*Noticing* CALAIH's *unenthusiastic reaction.*]

Do you not understand the proclamation, Calaih, Orphan of Joshua the Cow Herder?

CALAIH   I am to marry the High Lord on the last night of late winter.

MARDIAN   Yes, you have understood it well. How bright you are. And such fine hair. This proclamation shall now be taken to the Great Wall where all will read it and envy you your good fortune.

TARETTA   Wait. Are you certain there is no mistake?

MARDIAN   Mistake?

TARETTA   In the proclamation.

MARDIAN   There is no mistake Taretta, Orphan Whore of Joshua the Cow Herder. Good day now.

[MARDIAN *and the* GUARDS *exit.*]

TARETTA   So. I suppose you can gloat over this proclamation. You with your fine silver brush and comb.

CALAIH   What does the High Lord look like? Is he old or young?

TARETTA   Older than you—but not so old.

CALAIH   Do you remember the woman he set on fire?

TARETTA   Yes, Della—that ugly whore.

CALAIH   I remember how her flesh dripped off like thin wax and she was crying. I heard her crying coming from the flames.

TARETTA   Della—What an eyesore to the town she was, with her pox-marked face and hunched shoulders. They could burn all her kind for all I would care. Where are you going?

CALAIH   Outside, to sit with my cow.

[CALAIH *exits.*]

TARETTA   Very well. Go outside and sit with your cow. I am tired. My arm aches.

[*She sits rubbing her hand and arm.*]

· · · scene four · · ·

[*Afternoon, in the middle of winter, in the* APOTHECARY's *treatment room.*]

APOTHECARY   [*Finishing mixing his potion.*] The preparation is complete. Come in when you are ready. The wind is cold. I will have to put mortar in these cracks.

[*Takes bandages out.*]

Tell me about the wedding plans. How is it to have your sister betrothed to the High Lord?

[TARETTA *enters, with her arm covered in a cloth.*]

TARETTA   I pay you money, Apothecary, I expect a cure. Look at my arm; the bumps have grown. They are darker now and hard. At times I cannot move my arm for the pain it causes.

APOTHECARY   My potion soothes your pain, does it not, Taretta?

> [*Dips bandages into potion.*]

TARETTA   For a time, that is all, for a time.

APOTHECARY   Take down the cloth now.

[*She does so, and the* APOTHECARY *begins wrapping hot bandages around her arm. She flinches in pain.*]

> There. Think of something else for a moment and the burning will subside. Tell me about the wedding plans. How is it to have your sister betrothed to the High Lord?

TARETTA   Do not speak of it. It is of no use to me. My arm is burning. I cannot bear it. Take it off.

APOTHECARY   Here, lie back now. Lie back and breathe.

[*She lies back, breathing heavily.*]

> It is already the middle of winter. Just think, little Calaih will soon be moving to the castle of the High Lord.

TARETTA   Damn you; I said not to speak of it.

APOTHECARY   Very well, Taretta.

[*The* APOTHECARY *begins putting up potion and bandages.* TARETTA *lies back, taking deep breaths.*]

TARETTA Tell me, Apothecary—you have not told, have you? I pay you to keep your mouth shut.

APOTHECARY I have not told.

TARETTA Some of the men—they do not come anymore. They are not the same with me when I tell them I wear red velvet on my arms as they do in France, for the alluring…to be alluring. You do not tell them of my visits, Apothecary?

APOTHECARY No.

TARETTA Good. They must not find out. They must always fight to come to me. They must always want and love me.

APOTHECARY You can get dressed now, Taretta. Pay me my fee and go home.

TARETTA Yes. I will get dressed. One minute and I will get up and get dressed.

··· scene five ···

[*At night in midwinter by the stream and hillside.* CALAIH *sits wrapped in a thick shawl, despondently breaking sticks.* STEPHAN *enters carrying a satchel. She looks up at him and gasps.*]

STEPHAN Where is your cow?

CALAIH Down by the stream, licking stones in the water.

STEPHAN You are always with your cow.

CALAIH Where have you been? I go to the shop every day and ask for you, but they do not tell me where you have gone. I wait here with my cow every night in the cold. We look for you to come— but you do not come. Where have you been?

STEPHAN I have been away—on a journey. Why do you cry?

CALAIH Because I am so stupid. After that one night I thought you loved me, but then the next morning you go away.

STEPHAN Calaih, I am no fool. That morning I saw the proclamation. Your are to be wedded to the High Lord. He has sought you out and will give you finery and you will live in rich comfort and your children can eat gold every morning for breakfast if they wish. You will be happy.

CALAIH You believe that riches would make me so happy? That I would want all this gold and jewels and riches. I would scratch off the flesh from the High Lord's face. I would stab out the eyes of those fat children eating gold, if only you would not believe I would be wedded for riches.

STEPHAN I am sorry. I know you would not be.

CALAIH Tell me—

STEPHAN What?

CALAIH Do you want me?

STEPHAN Yes.

CALAIH For a wife?

STEPHAN Yes.

CALAIH I will go tell my cow.

STEPHAN Calaih, wait! You cannot marry me. It will be against the proclamation. I will not see you hurt.

CALAIH   He will not hurt me. He does not love me. He thinks my hair is beautiful. He sends a silver comb and brush saying, "For your beautiful long red hair, I worship it." What a noodle to worship hair. If he loves my hair, I will chip it off and send it to him in a box. But he shall not have me. I will go to the Letter Writer and have him send a message to the High Lord. I will say kindly that I cannot marry him as I am betrothed to Stephan the Shoemaker's Son.

STEPHAN   Would he accept such a letter?

CALAIH   I will make my mark on it.

STEPHAN   I have no sums of money or riches. I cannot even give you a betrothal ring.

CALAIH   Fine then. I do not like objects dangling on my fingers and arms.

STEPHAN   You do not?

CALAIH   No.

STEPHAN   Then would you take that star for your ring?

CALAIH   Which one?

STEPHAN   That small, very bright one.

CALAIH   The one up there?

STEPHAN   Yes.

CALAIH   If you give it to me, I will take it forever.

STEPHAN   I give it to you.

CALAIH   I will go tell my cow.

[*She exits. He follows her.*]

··· scene six ···

[*A cold morning in the middle of winter at the* LETTER WRITER's. *The* LETTER WRITER *sits behind his desk talking to* CALAIH.]

LETTER WRITER   You say you want to send a message to the High Lord?

CALAIH   Yes, that is what I want to do. But I have not learned how to do writing…so I come to you.

LETTER WRITER   Yes. I see. What kind of paper do you prefer?

CALAIH   Paper? It makes no difference.

LETTER WRITER   No difference. Certainly you do not want to send a message to the High Lord on coarse brown parchment. It would be an insult. You would appear a fool.

CALAIH   Something nice then. Something he would like.

LETTER WRITER   Let me see. I believe this elegant French scroll paper would be proper. It has a rich smooth texture with a colorful handpainted border. Here, you may touch it if you like.

CALAIH   Yes, it is very pretty.

LETTER WRITER   Now I believe gold ink is what you want. Any other would appear common on such fine paper as this.

[*Handing her a sheet of lettering.*]

Here, look at these lettering samples. See which you prefer.

CALAIH   [*Looking at lettering.*] I do not read—I cannot tell. Mmmm—this looks nice.

LETTER WRITER   Let me see. What! Block style? For a letter in gold ink to the High Lord? This is the lettering used when someone has lost a horse or a pig; this is the lettering used to denote the color of a cow's hide or the spots on swine. Block style is not something to be used on handpainted imported French scroll to be delivered to the High Lord.

CALAIH Very well then. You pick it out. I tell you I do not read. I do not know these different kinds of lettering and what is best. All I know is I have an important message that I must send right away to the High Lord, I do not know how to write so I come to you to write it for me. It is midwinter, my cow is waiting for me on the streets; he will be cold.

LETTER WRITER I am aware it is midwinter. I did not know you had a cow waiting for you on the streets. Tell me your message. I shall write it down quickly and recopy it later in a way I think suitable. I can have it delivered too if you want.

CALAIH Yes, do.

LETTER WRITER There will be an extra fee.

CALAIH Yes.

LETTER WRITER So, tell me—what is this message?

CALAIH Yes, the message. Let me see. Ah… Dear High Lord, I humbly thank you for your proposal to be wedded with me on the last night of late winter. Yet I tell you I am unable to accept this…engagement, as I am betrothed to Stephan the Shoemaker's Son. We are to be wedded in the early spring when he returns from Nalesca, where he is building a cottage for us both.

[*She stops, waiting for the* LETTER WRITER *to catch up. She then continues spontaneously.*]

In the village of Nalesca he will no longer be Stephan the Shoemaker's Son—but Stephan the Shoemaker, and I will be his wife, Calaih the Cow Herder.

[*Pause.*]

As you have expressed such fondness for my hair, I would be happy to cut it off and send it to you in a box. Please let me know your wishes. Your Humble Servant, Calaih, Orphan of Joshua the Cow Herder. There.

LETTER WRITER   Do you really want this sent?

CALAIH   Yes, it must be sent. You must send it.

LETTER WRITER   Very well then, make your mark.

[*She does so.*]

It will cost you a great deal. What with the fine paper and ink and lettering that you have chosen. It will cost perhaps more than a cow herder's orphan can pay.

CALAIH   [*Removing comb from her bag.*] Here is a silver comb for the payment. Look, there is even a design on it.

LETTER WRITER   Mmmm. Where did you get this?

CALAIH   It was a gift to me.

[*Pause, as he examines it suspiciously.*]

Look here, you may have this brush too, if you want.

[*He looks at the brush.*]

I would not want to keep it for myself—though Taretta might have liked it.

LETTER WRITER Mmmm. Very well. I will write up your letter as we have planned in exchange for this silver brush and comb.

CALAIH And deliver it too?

LETTER WRITER Yes, it will be delivered.

CALAIH Thank you. Good day.

LETTER WRITER [*As she is leaving.*] Yes, and good day to you too.

···scene seven···

[*Early evening on the last night of late winter in* TARETTA's *room above the tavern.* TARETTA *is wearing her seductive robe. Her hair is unkempt. She is sick and pale. Her arm is wrapped in red velvet.* ALEXTON *calls from outside.*]

ALEXTON [*Offstage.*] Taretta—

[*She starts, then begins dabbing perfume generously onto her arm.*]

TARETTA Yes, come in.

ALEXTON [*As he enters.*] Taretta—

TARETTA Ah, Alexton. You are early. It is not yet dark. You may get undressed if you like. It has been some time since I have chosen you. Forgive me, but I have been in great demand these past weeks.

[*Standing up weakly, supporting herself on the chair.*]

I will make it up to you though—you know I shall. Come, do my breasts still make you tremble?

[*He stares aghast, taking in her total dissipation.*]

So, show me the gifts you bring and we will begin.

ALEXTON   I have brought no gifts. You have not been in demand. No one has been coming here to you. They all say you are sick with a rotting disease.

TARETTA   Liars. They are liars.

ALEXTON   Why do you wear that red velvet on your arm?

TARETTA   I told you—it is the style of France.

ALEXTON   I do not believe you. Take it off and let me see.

[*Coming toward her, trying to grab hold of her arm.*]

Let me see your arm. Take this off! I insist—let me see—

TARETTA   Let go. Let go! Do not touch my arm.

[*She breaks away, trembling in pain.*]

ALEXTON   [*Recovering himself.*] Here is my advice to you, Taretta. Go to the Blacksmith's. He is skilled with an axe; his blades are sharp. He is quick and accurate. I tell you because, unlike the rest, I once cared something for you. I do not want to see you dead in the morning.

TARETTA   Get out.

ALEXTON   Yes, but before I go, I would like my wife's autumn head-dress. There has been no peace in my family since I gave it to you some time ago. My wife has beaten my dog to death with a stick, and we have been very miserable… I must have it back. I will pay you a fair price for it… Are you going to answer me?

TARETTA   Yes, I will get it—but you must do something for me.

You must tell them I am well, that they can come to me. Horace the Tavern Keeper, he will not let them up. In the mornings he tells me I am through, that they do not want to come. But that is a lie—he will not let them up. You go tell them. Get Casta the Miller—tell him I will bite and lick his big red ears, tell him that. And to Heilington make a noise like this, slurp, slurp, slurp, slurp… He will know what I mean, slurp, slurp.

ALEXTON   No one will come, Taretta—they know you are diseased and they have no use for you. Now give me the headdress and I will leave.

TARETTA   No use for me. No use for Taretta—the Woman of Flaming Nights!

ALEXTON   Taretta, the headdress.

TARETTA   Get out. You get out, you worm, or I will break this bottle across your mouth. You tell them to look for me when it turns dark.

[ALEXTON *leaves.*]

I have something for them to hear.

· · · scene eight · · ·

[*Early evening on the last night of late winter at the sisters' cottage. CALAIH is seated at the table sewing her wedding dress, eating cheese and singing. She finishes sewing, stands and puts the dress up to her, checking the fit. She continues to sing. MARDIAN enters with the two GUARDS behind her.*]

MARDIAN   Your hair is so lovely this evening. Are you ready to go?

CALAIH   What—

MARDIAN   Get your things together. It is time to go.

CALAIH   To go—

MARDIAN   Why do you stand so stunned? Is it not the last evening at the end of winter, the night of your marriage to the High Lord? Come, where are your things? Do you have anything to take.

CALAIH   No.

MARDIAN   The High Lord has asked me to see that you bring your silver brush and comb so that he may brush and comb out your fine hair late tonight.

CALAIH   I do not have them—they are lost—I have lost them.

MARDIAN   Indeed. How careless you were to lose them.

CALAIH   Yes.

MARDIAN   Well, come then. We must prepare you for the ceremony.

CALAIH   Did the High Lord not get my message?

MARDIAN   What?

CALAIH   I sent him a message. Do you not remember?

MARDIAN   A message?

CALAIH   Yes. After the message was sent, the marriage proclamation, they took it down from the Great Wall.

MARDIAN   Did they?

CALAIH   To have this proclamation taken down—does this not mean something?

MARDIAN   Nothing, perhaps, except the paper was worn and could not stand the strength and ice of the late winter's wind. Come now, there is much to be done before the ceremony.

[*She takes hold of* CALAIH*'s arm.*]

CALAIH Please, wait—he must have gotten my message—I took great trouble to send it properly. It was written on beautiful fine paper, the ink was real gold. It was to be delivered to him.

MARDIAN Perhaps there was such a message.

CALAIH Oh! So, he must know that tomorrow morning Stephan is returning from Nalesca, where he has built our home. We are to be married.

MARDIAN If the High Lord has received any such message, he has chosen to disregard it. Come. I can wait no longer. There is no time for further arguments.

[*She motions for* GUARDS. *They following speeches of* MARDIAN *and* CALAIH *occur simultaneously.*]

You must be cleaned and bathed and scrubbed with a brush. The dirt must come out of your nails and the wax from inside your ears. You must me powdered and perfumed and oiled and your hair must squeak and shine and be brushed and braided as the High Lord has demanded.

CALAIH [*As the* GUARDS *come for her.*] But the proclamation was taken down from the wall. No further announcements were made—I cannot go now—I have my own plans. Look, here is my wedding gown. That small bright star you see in the sky—it is my betrothal band—he gave it to me, it is mine—let go. Stop it— you are tearing my gown! Wait—let go of my hair! Ahh—I despise you! Stop! Stop! I will go then. I will go.

MARDIAN There now. Take her to the carriage.

CALAIH   Please—could I take my cow? I want my cow.

MARDIAN   I am sorry; but there is no room for a cow in your carriage.

[*The* GUARDS *lead out* CALAIH *as* MARDIAN *follows.*]

· · · scene nine · · ·

[*In the night on the last day of late winter at the tavern. Lights go up on* TARETTA, *who is covered with grotesque makeup and dressed in garish undergarments with red velvet wrapped around her.*]

TARETTA   So, you have no use for me. Alexton tells me that none of you have any more use for me. Is that so? Very well, but let me tell you too, that I have no need or use of you. Do you think I sit up in that room every night and wait for you to come to me— that I dress, adorn and perfume myself just to sit alone waiting— listening to your grunting noises below? Let me tell you that I do not sit long… I leave in the dark down the back stairway to the outside, to the meadows and the fields. There are many warm bulls and rams and beasts living in these hills and valleys. I have no need of human flesh. I enjoy the smell of the ram's rough fur. It arouses me. It is not so stale with sour ale and age, like the skin I bounced with above this tavern. It is warm and pure. I savor the taste and texture of dirt and hair in my teeth and nostrils; and the clutching of hooves on and at my breasts. The tongue of a bull is wet and thick wrapped all around my neck, as I lay on my belly holding tight to the twisting horns. Often the bulls have made me bleed and bleed until my gown and the ground are filled with dark blood. I turn on my back and stare up at the sky pressing my fingers over rocks, earth, roots. My God how I am satisfied. Finally; forever satisfied. I do not need you. I do not want you. Nothing you have can fill me.

···scene ten···

[*In the night on the last day of late winter in the dressing chamber at the castle of the* HIGH LORD. CALAIH *sits in a straight-back chair. Her long hair is braided. Her hands are tied.* MARDIAN *is standing over her, trimming the ribbons on her bridal headdress with silver shears.*]

MARDIAN   There—that will make it the right length. How Beautiful! Now I must tell you that the High Lord has heard of your behavior in the bath. It is distressing to him that you would scratch and bite that poor maiden's face. He wishes to speak with you before the ceremony. He would not like to see his bride binded up with ropes. I do not blame him.

[*She begins cutting ropes with shears.*]

I warn you, do not move from that chair. There are guards at the door.

[*She exits.* CALAIH *sits alone. The* HIGH LORD *enters. He is average looking and jovial. He is eating dried apricots.*]

HIGH LORD   Mmmmm—lovely, lovely, lovely. What hair. Tonight I will brush it out for you. Would you like that? Here, take a piece of fruit. An apricot. No?

[*He eats it himself.*]

So, they tell me you are unhappy—there was some unpleasantness in the bath. Let it pass, I say—let it pass. All we want is your happiness. Your happiness. I just wanted to make certain you knew that. How I stand in awe of your glorious tresses. They are glorious. Now tell me, have you any requests to make before the ceremony? Any at all?

CALAIH   Did you get my message?

HIGH LORD   Message?

CALAIH   Yes.

HIGH LORD   Yes. Yes, I received it. Thank you for thinking of me. The paper was exquisite, simply exquisite. The text of the letter was a bit disappointing as I recall, but then I am not marrying you under the pretense of any intellectual prowess. It is your hair I find so bewitching, enchanting. Now, if there is nothing more, I must leave you until the ceremony. Farewell. Wait, I will leave this fruit here, if you should chance to change your mind.

[*He places fruit on dresser and leaves. She looks at fruit, then catches sight of the shears. She grabs the shears and puts them down the front of her undergarment. MARDIAN enters with a robe.*]

MARDIAN   Here is your bridal robe. It is time to dress for the ceremony.

[*As she puts the robe on* CALAIH.]

Now you have met the High Lord, do you not see the foolishness in all your anguish and hysteria? He is handsome and jovial, is he not?

CALAIH   Yes, he is. We shall be very happy together.

· · · scene eleven · · ·

[*Late night in the late winter at the* BLACKSMITH'*s door.* TARETTA *is pale and shaking, her hair is wild. She wears a long cape wrapped tightly around her.*]

TARETTA   Let me in. Please, can I come in? I am sick. I need your help. I am freezing out here. I am dying. I tell you I am dying. Will you come—Blacksmith—will you come?

[BLACKSMITH *comes out.*]

Can you help me? I have heard that you are skilled with an axe. That your blades are sharp and your strokes are clean and accurate. I have need of such skills.

BLACKSMITH   And what have you brought for me to chop?

TARETTA   My arm, Blacksmith, my arm.

[*She holds up arm, then collapses. He carries her inside.*]

· · · scene twelve · · ·

[*In the late night of the late winter in the grand hall at the* HIGH LORD's *castle. Upstage, perhaps on a higher level, stands* MARDIAN, *the* APOTHECARY, *and one of the* GUARDS, *who wears a priest's robe. They all hold medallions. They are chanting. The* HIGH LORD *enters, and the chanting stops. He sits on his throne. There are several moments of silence, then music begins playing.* CALAIH *enters slowly in her bridal robe. The* HIGH LORD *smiles at her. She stops a few feet in front of him, grabs out the silver shears and cuts off her braid.*]

CALAIH   There is my fine hair that you want so much. It is dead now— dead like a crimson snake. I am glad. I hate it.

[*The* HIGH LORD *rises from his throne, steps forward and pulls the braid from between her fingers, kissing the braid longingly. Slowly, he looks up at her, then comes to her.*]

HIGH LORD   You stupid swine!

[*He grabs her by the shoulders, then begins biting off her ear.*]

··· scene twelve a ···

[*On another level in the background…the* BLACKSMITH *prepares for the removal of the arm… He brings* TARETTA *who is now delirious, sharpens blade, uncovers arm, and raises the blade on the* HIGH LORD's *line, "You stupid swine!" He swings and the lights dim to blackout as* CALAIH *and the* HIGH LORD *struggle and* TARETTA *screams. In the blackout, the screaming stops, and we hear the* HIGH LORD's *voice.*]

HIGH LORD'S VOICE   Here is your ear on the floor, if you want it.

··· scene thirteen ···

[*Early morning, the first day of spring at the sisters' cottage.* CALAIH *comes in. She is wearing the white undergarment and has a white cloth tied like a scarf around her head. The scarf is dark with blood on the side of her head where her ear has been removed. She carries a bloody handkerchief with her ear wrapped inside. She drops the handkerchief on the table and sits down. She is shaking with numbness. After a moment, she sees her wedding dress on the floor and goes to put it on. She is muttering to herself.*]

CALAIH   My cow. My cow. Why do they murder you? My cow, my
dear cow.

[*She has just gotten the torn dress on, though not hooked or buttoned, when* TARETTA *enters.* TARETTA's *face is white. With her one arm she holds her cape around her.*]

They let me go, Taretta. I am not to be burned. They let me go.

TARETTA   Yes, I see.

CALAIH   Did you see though—what they did to my cow—out there in
the yard?

TARETTA   I saw.

CALAIH   Help me get hooked, please. Stephan will be here soon. He will not mind about my ear. He cares so much for me. In time the hair will grow and cover it up. No, he will not mind about the ear. Please, hurry. Can you not use both hands?

TARETTA   Calaih, Stephan the Shoemaker's Son will not be coming here this morning.

CALAIH   Why? Did you see him?

[TARETTA *nods.*]

What did he tell you?

TARETTA   Nothing. He told me nothing. I only saw his head; it was dangling from on top of the pole outside the Great Wall.

CALAIH   Dead…dead…Stephan—dead.

[*She begins kissing her gown, then she begins tearing at it, ripping it off. Finally she throws it across the room and sits on the floor, holding and rocking herself.*]

I have nothing. Everything has been taken from me. Nothing.

TARETTA   Try not to despair, Little Calf. I too have had many things taken from me this evening.

CALAIH   What?

TARETTA   My arm. My arm was cut off.

CALAIH   Really? Was it cut off?

TARETTA   Without my arm there is no one who will want me. I have no work. No way to make money. I suppose I will have to live here forever.

CALAIH   So will I.

TARETTA   We will grow old together. In the winter we will eat hot porridge. You will feed berries to the birds, and I will learn to sew with one hand and teeth. I will always wear capes; short capes or long capes but always a cape to cover this nub.

CALAIH   I will keep my hair cropped off this way. I do not want it back.

TARETTA   It will be peaceful here.

CALAIH   I am sick with weariness.

TARETTA   If only we had the strength to sleep.

CALAIH   Yes, if I could only close my eyes for a moment.

[*She rocks back and forth.*]

Just for a moment…close my eyes.

[*They stare ahead as the lights fade. A tinny old blues song such as "Basin Street Blues" is heard playing in the distance.**]

• • •

*See Special Note on Songs and Recordings on copyright page.

The Yellow Wallpaper:

A dramatization of the short story by Charlotte Perkins Gilman

Adapted by Paul Kuritz

Paul Kuritz

A professor of theatre at Bates College, Paul Kuritz teaches acting and directing for the stage and camera. Since his directorial debut in 1966, Mr. Kuritz has directed over one hundred plays throughout the United States. In 1990 he was invited to teach and direct at the National Theater School in Bratislava, Slovakia. Mr. Kuritz is the author of *Fundamental Acting: A Practical Guide* (Applause Books, 1997), *The Making of Theatre History* (Prentice Hall, 1987), *Playing: An Introduction to Acting* (Prentice Hall, 1982), and *The Fiery Serpent*: *A Christian Theory of Film and Drama* (Pleasant Word, 2006). His most recent short film is *A New Life*.

characters

> SHE
>
> JOHN, her husband

time

> New England, 1891

setting

> A bedroom

ACT I

··· scene one ···

[*Light finds her in her room,* JOHN *has just exited. Bed in upper right corner, chair and writing desk upper left, exit upper left.* SHE *notices the audience and begins to talk about her house.*]

SHE   Ancestral halls…
     A colonial mansion,
     An hereditary estate.

> [*Aside.*] I would say a haunted house, and reach the height of romantic felicity—but that would be asking too much of fate! Still! There is something queer about it.
> Else, why should it be let so cheaply? And why have stood so long "untenanted"?

JOHN   [*Enters, puts shawl around her, exits.*]

SHE   John laughs at me. But one expects that in marriage.

> John is practical in the extreme. He has no patience with faith [*lifting her Bible*], an intense horror of superstition, and he scoffs openly at any talk of things not to be felt and seen and put down in figures.

John is a physician. And perhaps, perhaps that is one reason I do not "get well" faster.

You see: He does not believe I am sick! So what can I do?

If a physician of high standing, and one's own husband, assures friends and relatives that there is really nothing the matter with me but "temporary nervous depression—a slight hysterical tendency."

What can I do?

[*Looking at photo in a frame on wall by bed.*]

My brother is also a physician. Also of high standing. And he says the same thing.

[*Picking up pill containers and lines them up on the floor.*]

So I take phosphates.

Phosphites, Tonics, and journeys, and air, and exercise, and am absolutely forbidden to "work" until I am well again.

Personally, I disagree with their ideas.

Personally, I believe that work, excitement and change, would do me good.

But what can I do?

[*Picking up and looking through papers, laying them one by one behind the row of pill and tonic containers.*]

I did write for a while in spite of them.

But it exhausts. Having to be so sly about it.

I sometimes fancy that in my condition if I had less opposition and more society and stimulus—but John says

JOHN   [*Enters, collects papers, pill and tonic containers, and puts them away.*]

The very worst thing you can do is to think about your condition.

SHE   I confess it always makes me feel bad.

[JOHN *exits.*]

So I will let it alone.
And talk about the house.
The most beautiful place! It is quite alone, standing well back from the road, quite three miles from the village. There is a delicious garden.

There were greenhouses, too, but they are all broken now.
The place has been empty for years.
There is something strange about the house.
I can feel it.
I even said so to John, but he said

JOHN   [*Enters.*] What you felt was a draught.

[*He shuts the window and exits.*]

SHE   And he shut the window!
I get angry with John sometimes.
I never used to be so sensitive.
I think it is due to this nervous condition.
But John says

JOHN   [*Enters, calms her.*] If you feel so, you will neglect proper self-control.

[*Exits.*]

SHE   So I control myself.
And that makes me very tired.
I don't like this room a bit.
I wanted one downstairs that opened on the piazza and had roses all over the window, and such pretty old-fashioned chintz hangings!

But John would not hear of it.

JOHN   [*Enters.*] There was only one window and not room for two beds, and no near room for me if I took another.

SHE   He is very careful and loving.
He hardly lets me stir without special direction.
I have a schedule prescription for each hour in the day.
He takes care of me.
So I feel ungrateful not to value it more.

JOHN   We came here solely on your account.
You are to have perfect rest and all the air you can get.
Your exercise depends on your strength, my dear.
And your food somewhat on your appetite.
But air you can absorb all the time.

[*Exits.*]

SHE   So we took this—the nursery at the top of the house.
It is a big, airy room, the whole floor nearly.

It was nursery first and then playroom and gymnasium: the windows are barred for little children, and there are rings and things in the walls.

The paint and paper look as if a boys' school had used it. It is stripped off in great patches all around the head of my bed, about as far as I can reach, and in a great place on the other side of the room low down.

I never saw a worse paper.
No wonder the children hated it!
I'd hate it myself if I had to live in this room long.
There comes John.

I must stop.

[*Lights out and up.*]

SHE [*Sitting with pen and paper in hand, reading what* SHE *has written and is writing.*]

"We have been here two weeks now and I haven't felt like writing before, since that first day. I am sitting by the window now, up in this atrocious nursery, and there is nothing to hinder my writing as much as I please, save lack of strength."

[*Rises and crosses to center.*]

John is away all day, and even some nights when his cases are serious.
I am glad my case is not serious!
But these nervous troubles are dreadfully depressing.
John does not know how much I suffer.
He knows there is no reason to suffer.
And that satisfies him.
Of course it is only nervousness.
But it weighs on me not to do my duty in any way!
I meant to be such a help to John—a real rest and comfort.
And here I am a burden.
Already!
Nobody believes what an effort it is to do what little I can: — to dress and entertain, and order things.

It is fortunate Mary is so good with the baby.
Such a dear baby!
And yet I cannot be with him.
It makes me too nervous.
I suppose John never was nervous.
He laughs at me about this wallpaper!
At first he meant to repaper the room, but afterwards he said

JOHN [*Enters, takes her writing material away.*]

You are letting it get the better of you.
Nothing is worse for a nervous patient than to give way to such fancies.
After the wallpaper was changed it would be the heavy bedstead, and then the barred windows, and then that gate at the head of the stairs, and so on.
You know the place is doing you good.
And really, dear, I don't care to renovate the house just for three months.

SHE [*Desperate, pleading.*] Then let's go downstairs.

There are such pretty rooms there.

JOHN [*Taking her in his arms.*] You blessed little goose!

[*Exits.*]

SHE [*Crushed. Beat. Begins to talk herself into a better mood.*]

He is right about the beds and windows and things.
It is an airy and comfortable room.
And, of course, I would not want to make him uncomfortable just for a whim.
I'm really getting quite fond of this big room.
All but this horrid paper.

[*Crosses to window.*]

At least I can see the garden: those mysterious deep-shaded arbors, the riotous old-fashioned flowers, and bushes and gnarly trees.

[*Crosses to other window.*]

And I get a lovely view of the bay and a little private wharf belonging to the estate.

There is a beautiful shaded lane that runs down there from the house.

I always fancy I see people walking in these paths and arbors.

But John has cautioned me

JOHN   [*Enters.*] Do not give way to fancy in the least.

With your imaginative power and habit of story-making, a nervous weakness like yours is sure to lead to all manner of excited fancies.

You ought to use your will and good sense to check the tendency.

[*Exits.*]

SHE   [*Crushed again.*] So I try.

[*Pause. She starts for the writing table.*]

If I were only well enough to write a little it would relieve the press of ideas and rest me. But I get pretty tired when I try. It is so discouraging not to have any advice and companionship.

JOHN   [*Enters.*]

When you get really well, we will ask Cousin Henry and Julia down for along visit.

[*Lifts up the pillow on her bed, making a joke.*]

But I would as soon put fireworks in your pillow-case as to let you have those stimulating people about now.

[*Exits.*]

SHE [*Starts after him.*] I wish I could get well faster.

[*Turns back.*]

But I must not think about that. This paper looks to me as if it knew what a vicious influence it had!

[*Seeing as if for the first time, a major discovery. Perhaps* SHE *begins to project onto the paper the feelings for* JOHN *she can't or won't admit.*]

There is a recurrent spot where the pattern looks like a broken neck.
And two bulbous eyes stare at you upside down.
The impertinence of it!
And the everlastingness!
Up and down and sideways they crawl.
And those absurd, unblinking eyes are everywhere.

[*Discovers a particular wallpaper seam for the first time and inspects it.*]

There is one place where tow breadths don't match.
The eyes go all up and down the line, one a little higher than the other.
I never saw so much expression in an inanimate thing before.

[*Backs away from it toward bed.*]

[*Lies on the bed.*]

I used to lie awake as a child and get more entertainment and terror out of blank walls and plain furniture than most children could find in a toy store.

I remember what a kindly wink the knobs of our big, old bureau used to have.

There [*notices her writing chair*] was one chair that always seemed like a strong friend. I used to feel that if any of the other things looked too fierce I could always hop into that chair and be safe.

[SHE *does so.*]

[*Pause.*]

[SHE *notices the paper beside her.*]

This wallpaper, as I said before, is torn off in spots. It sticks closer than a brother.

[*Noticing the floor for the first time.*]

The floor is scratched

[*Walking and examining each thing* SHE *notices empathetically.*]

and gouged and splintered.

[*Looking at the ceiling.*]

The plaster is dug out here and there.

[*At her bed.*]

And this great heavy bed looks as if it had been through the wars. But I don't mind it a bit—only the paper.

[*Offstage sounds of trays of dishes being dropped.*]

There comes John's sister.

[*Sarcastically.*] Such a dear girl.
And so careful of me!
I must not let her find me writing.
She is a perfect and enthusiastic housekeeper, who hopes for no
better profession.
She probably thinks the writing made me sick!
But I write when she is out,

[*Crossing to her writing desk.*]

and see her a long way off from these windows.

[*Crossing to window.*]

This is one that commands the road.

[*Noticing the wallpaper, as if discovering something very important about
it for the first time.*]

This wallpaper has a kind of sub-pattern in a different shade, a
particularly irritating one. You can only see it in certain lights.

[*Gets candle, lights it, and uses it to examine the wallpaper more closely.*]

And not clearly then.
But in the places where it isn't faded and where the sun is just
so—
I can see a strange, provoking, formless sort of figure.
It seems to skulk about behind that silly and conspicuous front
design.

[*Sound of a tray of dishes dropped.*]

There's sister on the stairs!

[*Lights down and up.*]

SHE   [SHE *has a small American flag to wave.*]

Well, the Fourth of July is over!
The people are all gone.
And I am tired out.

[*Sits on the bed.*]

John thought it might do me good to see a little company.
So we just had mother and Nellie and the children down for a
week.
Of course I didn't do a thing.

[*Bitterly.*] Jennie sees to everything now.
But it tired me all the same.

JOHN   [*Enters.*] If you don't pick up faster I shall send you to Weir
Mitchell in the fall.

SHE   But I don't want to go there at all. I had a friend who was in his
hands once.

[JOHN *exits.*]

And she says he is just like John and my brother, only more so!
Besides, it is such an undertaking to go so far.
I don't feel that it is worth it.

[*Fighting back tears.*]

I cry at nothing. And cry most of the time.
Of course I don't when John is here or anybody else.
But when I am alone….
And I am alone a good deal just now.
John is kept in town very often by "serious cases."

And Jennie is good and lets me alone when I want her to.

[*Trying to talk herself into believing it to be true.*]

I'm getting really fond of the room in spite of the wallpaper.
Perhaps because of the wallpaper. It dwells in my mind so!
I lie here on this great immovable bed—it is nailed down, I
believe—and follow that pattern about by the hour.
It is as good as gymnastics.
I start at the bottom, down in the corner over there where it has
not been touched, and I determine for the thousandth time to
follow that pointless pattern to some sort of a conclusion.
But, on the other hand, they connect diagonally.
And the sprawling outlines run off in great slanting waves of
optic horror.
The whole thing goes horizontally, too.
At least it seems so.
It makes me tired to follow it. I will take a nap I guess.

[*Lights fade and up.*]

SHE   I don't know why I should say this.

[*Starts, but decides against it.*]

I don't want to.

[*Again starts, but can't.*]

I don't feel able.
And I know John would think it absurd.
But I must say what I feel and think some how.

[*Tries again, fails again.*]

The effort is getting to be greater than the relief.
Half the time now I am awfully lazy, and lie down ever so much.

JOHN   [*Enters.*] You mustn't lose your strength.

[*Gets her medicine, gives it to her.*]

SHE   [*To the audience, as if* JOHN *weren't there.*]

> He has me take cod liver oil.
> And lots of tonics and things.
> To say nothing of ale and wine and rare meat.
> Dear John!
> He loves me very dearly.
> He hates to have me sick.
> I tried to have a real earnest reasonable talk with him the other day:
> Let me go and visit Cousin Henry and Julia.

JOHN   You aren't able to go.
> Nor able to stand it after you got there.

SHE   I did not make a very good case for myself.
> I was crying before I finished.
> It is getting to be a great effort to think straight.
>
> Just this "nervous weakness" I suppose.
> And dear John gathers me up in his arms.

[JOHN *does so*].

> And just lays me on the bed, and sits by me, and reads to me till it tires my head.

JOHN   You are my darling and my comfort and all I have.
> You must take care of yourself. For my sake.
> And keep well. No one but you can help you out of this.
> Use your will and self-control.
> Don't let any silly fancies run away with you.

[*He exits.*]

SHE There are things in this paper that nobody knows but me. Or ever
will.
Behind the outside pattern the dim shapes get clearer every day.
It is always the same shape, only very numerous.
And it is like—a woman, stooping down and creeping about
behind that pattern.
I don't like it a bit.
I wonder…
I think…
I wish John would take me away from here!

[*Lights fade and up.*]

[JOHN *asleep onstage.*]

SHE It is so hard to talk to John about my case.
He is so wise, he loves me so…
But I tried it last night.

It was moonlight.
The moon shines in all around.
I hate to see it sometimes, it creeps so slowly.
John was asleep and I hated to wake him.
So I kept still and watched the moonlight on that undulating
wallpaper till I felt creepy.

[*Sees the figure shaking the paper for the first time.*]

The faint figure behind seems to be shaking the pattern. As if she
wants to get out.
I got up softly and went to feel and see if the paper did move.
And when I came back—John was awake.

JOHN   What is it, little girl?
Don't go walking about like that.
You'll get cold.

SHE   I really am not gaining here.
I want you to take me away.

JOHN   Why, darling, our lease will be up in three weeks.
I can't see how to leave before.
The repairs are not done at home.
I cannot possibly leave town just now.
Of course if you were in any danger, I could and would.
But you really are better, dear, whether you can see it or not.
I am a doctor, dear, and I know. You are gaining flesh and color.
Your appetite is better. I feel really much better about you.

SHE   I don't weigh a bit more, nor even as much.
My appetite may be better in the evening when you are here, but
it is worse in the morning when you are away!

JOHN   Bless your little heart.

[*He hugs her.*]

You'll be as sick as you please!
But now let's go to sleep, and talk about it in the morning!

SHE   [*Gloomily.*] You won't go away?

JOHN   Why, how can I, dear?
It is only three weeks more. Then we will take a nice little trip
for a few days while Jennie is getting the house ready. Really,
dear, you are better!

SHE   Better in body perhaps—

[JOHN *sits up straight and looks at her with a stern, reproachful look.*]

JOHN   My darling, I beg of you, for my sake and for our child's sake, as well as for your own, never, even for one instant, let that idea enter your mind!

There is nothing as dangerous, as fascinating, to a temperament like yours. It is a false and foolish fancy. Can't you at least trust me as a physician?

[*Her silence answers him and he exits.*]

SHE   I said no more on that score.
He thought I was asleep.
But I wasn't.
I lay there for hours trying to decide whether the front pattern and the back pattern move together or separately.

[*Lights fade and up.*]

SHE   There is one marked peculiarity about this paper.

A thing nobody seems to notice but myself.
It changes as the light changes.

[JOHN *enters manipulating gossamer puppet of Woman Behind the Wall, and he slowly, slowly circles her along the four walls of the room.*]

The outside pattern, and the woman behind it, is as plain as can be.
I didn't realize for a long time what the thing was that showed behind, that dim sub-pattern. But now I am quite sure.
It is a woman. By daylight she is subdued, quiet. It is so puzzling. The fact is

[SHE *starts to say it, hesitates, but this time succeeds.*]

I am getting a little afraid of John. He seems very queer sometimes.

Even Jennie has an inexplicable look. It must be the paper!

I have watched John when he did not know I was looking.

I've caught him several times looking at the paper!

And Jennie too: I caught her with her hand on it once.

She asked me why I should frighten her so!

Then she said that the paper stained everything it touched, that
she had found yellow smooches on all my clothes and John's, and
she wished we would be more careful!

So innocent!

I know she was studying that pattern.

[*Vows.*]

But nobody will find it out but me!

[*Lights fade and up.*]

SHE   Life is very much more exciting now than it used to be.

You see I have something more to expect, to look forward to, to
watch.

I really do eat better.

And am more quiet than I was.

[JOHN *enters.*]

John is so pleased to see me improve!

He laughed a little the other day, and said

JOHN   You seem to be flourishing *in spite* of your wallpaper.

SHE   [*Laughs.*] I had no intention of telling him it was *because of* the
wallpaper.

He would make fun of me.

He might even want to take me away.
I won't leave now until I have found it out!
One week more!

[*Lights fade and up.*]

SHE   I'm feeling ever so much better! I don't sleep much at night. I
watch—developments.
There is something else about that paper—the smell!
I noticed it the moment we came into the room. But with so
much air and sun it was not bad. And whether the windows are
open or not, the smell is here.
It creeps all over the house. It gets into my hair.
Such a peculiar odor, too!

It is not bad—at first, and very gentle, but quite the subtlest,
most enduring odor I ever met. It used to disturb me at first. I
thought of burning the house.

But now I am used to it.
The only thing I can think of that it is like is the color of the
paper!
A yellow smell.
There is a very funny mark on this wall, low down, near the
mop-board. A streak that runs round the room. It goes behind
every piece of furniture.

Except the bed.
A long, straight, even smooch. As if it had been rubbed over and
over.
I wonder how it was done. Who did it. What they did it for.
Round and round and round and round and round and round…

[*Dizzy, falls into the bed.*]

[*Lights fade and up.*]

SHE   [JOHN *is now himself the gossamer figure moving around the room's perimeter.*]

I discovered something. I found out.
The front pattern moves!
The woman behind shakes it!
Sometimes I see many women behind.
Sometimes only one.
She crawls around fast, and her crawling shakes it all over.
She is all the time trying to climb through.
But nobody could climb through that pattern—it strangles so.
If that head were only covered or cut…

[*Lights fade and up.*]

SHE   I think she leaves in the daytime! I've seen her!
I can see her out of every one of my windows!
It is the same woman.

[*Looking at one window.*]

I see her in that long shaded lane, creeping up and down.

[*Looking at the other window.*]

I see her in those dark grape arbors, creeping all around the garden.

[*Back at the first window.*]

I see her on that long road under thee trees, creeping along.
I don't blame her a bit. I always lock the door when I creep.
I don't do it at night. John would suspect something.
And John is so queer now. I don't want to irritate him.
I wish he would take another room!

Besides, I don't want anybody else to get that woman but myself!

[*Lights fade and up.*]

SHE   I have found out another funny thing.
     But I won't tell you this time!
     I can't trust you with too much.
     There are only two more days to get this paper off.
     John is beginning to notice.
     I don't like the look in his eyes.
     John knows I don't sleep very well at night.
     He asks me all sorts of questions, too, and pretends to be very
     loving and kind.
     As if I can't see through him!

[*Lights fade and up.*]

SHE   Hurrah! This is the last day.
     John is staying in town overnight, and won't be out until this
     evening.
     Last evening, as soon as it was moonlight, that poor thing began
     to crawl and shake the pattern.
     I got up and ran to help her.
     I pulled, she shook. I shook, she pulled.
     Before morning we had peeled off yards of this paper.

     [SHE *reveals a bucket of yellow strips of paper.*]

     And when the sun came that awful pattern began to laugh at
     me—

     [*Laughs at the paper in the bucket.*]

     I will finish you to-day!
     We are going away to-morrow.

Jennie was amazed, but I told her merrily that I did it out of pure spite.

She laughed and said she wouldn't mind doing it herself.

[*To the bucket of paper.*]

But nobody touches you but me! Not alive, anyway.
She tried to get me out of the room.

[*Lies down on bed.*]

But I said that I believed I would lie down again and sleep all I could; and not to wake me even for dinner. I would call when I woke.

Now she's gone.
The servants are gone.
The things are gone. And there is nothing left.
But I must get to work.
I have locked the door and thrown the key down into the front path.

I don't want to go out, and I don't want anybody to come in.
Till John comes.
I want to astonish him.

[SHE *takes rope with noose from a secret place, perhaps the rope used to manipulate the gossamer figure.*]

I've got a rope that even Jennie did not find.
If this woman does get out, and tries to get away, I can tie her!
I am getting angry enough to do something desperate. To jump out of the window would be admirable exercise, but the bars are too strong even to try.
Besides I wouldn't do it. Of course not.
"People don't do such things!"
I don't even like to look out of the windows—there are so many

of those creeping women, and they creep so fast.
I wonder if they all come out of you as I did?

[*Ties end of rope to bed leg and puts noose around her neck.*]

But I am securely fastened now. You won't get me out in the road there!

I suppose I shall have to get back behind the pattern tonight.

That is hard!

It is so pleasant to be out in this great room and creep around as I please!

I don't want to go outside.

[*Sits on floor.*]

I won't.

[*Hears something we can't hear.*]

Why there's John at the door!
Calling and pounding!
Now he's crying for an axe.
It would be a shame to break down that beautiful door!
"John dear, the key is down by the front steps."

[*Listens again.*]

That silenced him for a few moments.

JOHN   Open the door, my darling.

SHE   I can't. The key is down by the front door.

[SHE *repeats it again, several times, very gently and slowly.*]

JOHN   What is the matter? For God's sake, what are you doing!

SHE   I'll just keep on creeping.
        I've got out at last.
        In spite of you.
        And I've pulled off most of the paper.
        So you can't put me back in!

        [*Listens. Then to audience.*]

        Did he faint?
        So now I have to creep over him!

[*Blackout as* SHE *creeps up and out.*]

• • •

In Bed
with Kafka/
Kafka in Bed

Neena Beber

Neena Beber

Neena Beber's plays include *Jump/Cut*, *The Dew Point*, *Hard Feelings*, *Thirst*, *A Common Vision*, *Tomorrowland*, *The Brief but Exemplary Life of the Living Goddess*, *Failure to Thrive*, and a children's play, *Zachariah Mosely's Neon Blues*. She is the recipient of an Obie Grant, the L. Arnold Weissberger Award, and an A.S.K. Exchange to the Royal Court Theatre in London, as well as grants from AT&T and the NEA, commissions from Playwrights Horizons and Otterbein College, a Sloan Commission from Cleveland Playhouse, and Paulette Goddard and MacDowell Colony Fellowship. Theatres that have premiered her work include the Women's Project, Theater J, Woolly Mammoth, the Magic Theatre, New Georges, Thick Description, the Humana Festival, Gloucester Stage, Padua Hills Playwrights Festival, and SPF. Other one-acts include *Misreadings*, *A Body of Water*, *Sensation(s)*, *Adaptive Ruse*, *After Thought*, and *Help*. She was recently a member of New Dramatists and HB Playwrights Unit and currently a member of New York Playwrights Lab. Ms. Beber has contributed articles to *American Theatre*, *Theatre*, and *Performing Arts Journal*, and her fiction has been published in *The Sun*. Her writing for children's television has garnered several Emmy and Cable Ace Award nominations. She received a B.A. from Harvard University and an M.F.A. from N.Y.U.'s Dramatic Writing Program.

··· **production note** ···

In Bed with Kafka/Kafla in Bed was first produced by HB Playwrights Festival, founder and artistic director William Carden, and directed by Marya Cohn with the following cast: Larry Block (Dr. X), Gary Brownlee (K), and Laura Flanagan (F).

The play is dedicated to Adrienne Shelly with gratitude, love, and fond memory.

Note: Franz Kafka died of tuberculosis in 1924 at age 41. Soon after World War II, tuberculosis was considered effectively cured. During the war, Kafka's three sisters were killed in concentration camps; his great love, Felice Bauer, escaped to Switzerland, and died in the United States in her seventies. The pace of the play is intended to be farcical, with rapid entrances and exits by Dr. X.

[*A hospital room.* K *lies in a hospital bed.* F *sits in a nearby chair.* DR. X *stands with a clipboard.*]

DR. X   We have good news and bad news.

K   The bad news first.

DR. X   You're dying.

K   What is the good news?

DR. X   A cure will be found for your disease.

K   When?

DR. X   Ten years.

K   How long do I have?

DR. X   Six months.

K   Then the good news evades me.

DR. X   You have hit upon it, haven't you.

[DR. X *goes.* F *gets into the bed.*]

F   Let's switch places.

K   Why?

F   It should be me instead of you.

K   Why?

F   I am interested in draperies. That is my profound interest. To choose the draperies that will hang above the window. To choose the color that will curtain my view. To live comfortably and with color.

K   You will attain what you desire and so your life is possible.

F   Move over.

K   Why do you want to die?

F   I don't. But I want you to live.

K   We don't get to switch.

F   Why not?

K   The rules don't work that way.

F   What if they do?

[DR. X *appears.*]

DR. X   There is good news and bad.

F   The good news first please.

K   That's where we differ.

DR. X   The good news is that—I'm sorry. I was wrong. There is no good news.

F   What is the bad news?

DR. X   That is the bad news.

[DR. X *goes.* K *and* F *look at each other.*]

K   You know that I've always loved you.

F   I've always suspected that I would age badly.

K   Thank you for saying that.

[DR. X *appears.*]

DR. X   You're in luck. I've thought of something.

[K *and* F *look at him.*]

DR. X   Some terrible things are going to happen and you won't be
around to see them.

F   Which one of us are you talking to?

K   She doesn't understand that I'm alone in this.

DR. X   [*To* F.] Aha, there you are: the good news is that you'll die of a
disease that seventy-five years later still has no cure. The bad
news is that it will take seventy-five years to kill you.

K   I think you've got it backwards. Which is the good news and which is
the bad.

DR. X   Perhaps I do.

[DR. X *goes.*]

F   I'm dying so slowly then. Everything I do takes me forever. You're
the fast study.

K   The good news is that I was planning to starve myself to death and
now I don't have to.

[DR. X *appears. He starts to speak, gets confused, goes.*]

F   The good news is that your letters will be worth more to me.

K   The bad news is that when I ask you to burn them, you won't listen.

F   The bad news is that your letters will be worth more to me.

[DR. X *appears.*]

DR. X   Switch places.

F I told you so.

DR. X It's my turn.

[DR. X *gets into the hospital bed. He pushes F and K out.*]

DR. X The bad news is that seventy-five years can pass very quickly.

K It all evens out in the end.

F Is that good news or bad news?

K I don't know.

F Think about it and tell me tomorrow.

K When I wake up I'll be somebody else.

F Is that a fear or a hope?

K I've never loved anybody else.

F Is that good news or bad news?

K I don't know.

DR. X A hospital is no place to be well.

F Dance with me.

K You can't imagine that I would ever dance.

DR. X I can.

K All right then. I shall dance.

[*Music.* F *and* K *dance, swirling around the room. As their pace quickens:*]

DR. X They dance. They switch places. They dance. They switch places. They dance. They switch places. Somebody has changed the rules without asking. Dizzy. Dizzy. What am I doing in this bed?

[F *and* K *stop dancing abruptly. Music cuts off.* F *and* K *come around the hospital bed with flowers.*]

F   We're sorry you're not well.

DR. X   I thank you for your sentiments.

K   We never thought it would happen to you.

DR. X   I could use some more pain killer.

F   I'll ring for the doctor.

DR. X   I'm the doctor.

F   Another one then.

[F *goes.*]

K   It isn't our fault.

DR. X   That's what they all say.

K   I take full responsibility.

DR. X   Very few do these days.

K   I mean what I say this time.

DR. X   The bad news is that you are already dead.

K   A slight exaggeration.

[F *returns, wearing a nurse's cap.*]

F   I couldn't find a soul.

K   That doesn't surprise me. I looked for one for years…

DR. X   You're the nurse now?

F   I thought it might suit me.

K   I must ask everyone to leave me alone.

F   [*As she and* DR. X *start to go.*] When were you otherwise?

K   She's right, of course; don't go!

F   Visiting hours are over.

DR. X   Who made the rules?

F   Didn't you?

[F *exits again as* K *gets back into the hospital bed.*]

K   Switch places.

DR. X   I can't.

K   Switch places.

DR. X   I won't.

K   Switch places.

DR. X   I have no place.

K   Have you ever cured anything in your life?

DR. X   I might have. No one lives to tell me about it.

K   You're no different.

DR. X   Than whom?

K   Than yourself.

DR. X   Good news. Six months to do as you please. You can stay here or you can go. If I were you I'd—

K   You're not!

DR. X   No. I'm not, am I.

[DR. X *disappears.* K *is left alone. He rings a bell and calls out.*]

K   Doctor! My head! Something for my head! Please bring me something for my head!

. . .

El Depresso
Espresso

Laura Shaine Cunningham

Laura Shaine Cunningham

Laura Shaine Cunningham is a playwright, journalist, and author of seven books. Ms. Cunningham's fiction and non-fiction have appeared in the *New Yorker* and the *New York Times*. She has written seven full-length plays, including *Sleeping Arrangements*, *Beautiful Bodies*, and *Bang*. She is widely produced, and has several other short plays in the Vintage anthologies *Take Ten*, *Take Ten II*, and *Leading Women*. *Sleeping Arrangements* had its world premiere January 2007 at Theater J in Washington, D.C.

characters

MO   A man, youngish, very depressed (should be able to do Irish inflection, slight)

LIV   A woman, youngish, very depressed (should be able to do Jewish inflection, slight)

DR. YOSHIMURA   Handsome Japanese doctor

DR. OBOLENSKI   Beautiful Russian doctor

props

Draped coffee cart: Starbucks containers

music

Cajun, Zydeco cassettes

• • •

[*Scene: The Depression Clinic of a well-known New York City Hospital. Midnight. A drizzly, dreary spring night. Outside, police and ambulance sirens shrill the call of the city-wild. The sterile room has a sign: "Yoshimura-Obolenski Depression Clinic." There are a row of plain chairs, a movable screen, and a draped medical cart. As the lights come up, we see MO, a depressed young man, slumped in his chair, a crumpled cigarette pack in his hand. His head is low, his hands drag toward the floor. He occasionally fondles himself. He is in a deep melancholia. LIV, a young woman, also depressed, enters, in a tentative, diffident manner, backs out, reenters, finally addresses MO. She holds a newspaper advertisement, crumpled in her hand, and also a pack of cigarettes.*]

LIV   Is…is this…the right place?

     [MO *doesn't respond.*]

LIV   [*Continues.*]

     Is…Is this the Yoshimura-Obolenski Depression Clinic?

I saw the ad.

[*She reads crumpled newspaper.*]

"Have your eating and sleeping habits changed? Have you gained or lost weight?

"Do you start to cry for no reason?

[*She sniffles.*]

"If you have answered 'yes' to any of the above questions, you may be eligible for a new and innovative treatment program that begins tonight, at midnight at the Yoshimura-Obolenski Depression Clinic. You will be paid for your participation." So…is this it?

[MO *doesn't respond.*]

LIV   Why did I get out of bed? I should just go home… Now, I'll have to wait hours for the Second Avenue bus. They say it comes every twenty-two minutes after midnight, but they are lying. Oh, the hell with it, I'll take the subway. Oh, why don't I just throw myself onto the tracks? And now the fare has gone up. A twenty-dollar fare card and it's all a waste. My fare cards are expired anyway…trips I never took.

    [*She sniffles.*]

MO   [*Without lifting his head.*] Can't you read? There's a sign.

LIV   [*Reading the sign.*] Oh, well, now I feel stupid.

    [*She sits down, slumps beside* MO.]

    [*He reacts, ever so slightly inching away.*]

MO   Do you mind?

LIV   What?

MO   I don't like people…touching me. It gives me the heebie-jeebies.

[*She inches away.*]

LIV   I'm sorry. I'm sorry. Yeah, yeah, I'm so sorry, sorry I'm alive.

MO   Yeah.

LIV   So where's the doctors? The ad says "Anti-Depression Team." Innovative New Three Pronged Treatment for Depression.

MO   How would I know?

[*At that moment, we hear the clicketty clack of brisk steps and white lab-coated* DR. YOSHIMURA *and* DR. OBOLENSKI *enter.* DR. YOSHIMURA *is a handsome man and* DR. OBOLENSKI *is a stunning woman.*]

DR. YOSHIMURA   Hi! We're so glad…you've…

DR. OBOLENSKI   Chosen to attend our clinic…

MO   I said "I'd *see.*"

LIV   You don't have to pay me to participate. You know, maybe this is a mistake. I don't like the lighting…too bright. I don't like the color scheme either. Or the feel of the chairs. Or this… other…individual… [*She indicates* MO.] I think I'll wait for the bus after all…

DR. YOSHIMURA   [*Whispers to* DR. OBOLENSKI.] Correct his thinking…I'll deal with her…

[*Each* DOCTOR *flanks a patient, consolingly.*]

[*Dialogue may overlap.*]

DR. YOSHIMURA   [*To* LIV.] So tell me…

[*He looks at a card.*]

Liv. Have you experienced changes in your sleeping pattern?

LIV   Yes. I used to sleep eighteen hours a day, now it's twenty-three. I'm wearing my nightgown under this raincoat.

DR. OBOLENSKI   [*To* MO.] Mo, may I call you that?

MO   I don't care what you call me.

DR. OBOLENSKI   I love the name "Mo"… Short for Morton? Or Mohammed?

MO   I dunno. My parents abandoned me after a few years of abuse. They just used to say, I don't want you no *mo*. The name stuck.

DR. OBOLENSKI   So, Mo, change in weight…up or down?

MO   I feel a disgusting subcutaneous layer of fat and gristle all over my body, double roll folds over my belly when I sit on the toilet, which is almost all the time. The single thing that comforts me is smoking…and they won't let me light up in here…

DR. YOSHIMURA   [*To* LIV.] And have you noticed a change in your appetite?

LIV   Yes, it's worse. I want to eat things that are bad for me. Mostly donut holes, and Ranchero spicy chips—I know people say I'm thin, even skinny but when I look in the mirror I see a fat, humongous blob… I wish I could smoke.

DR. OBOLENSKI   [*To* MO.] How many times a day do you masturbate?

MO   Whad do you want to know?

DR. OBOLENSKI   It's an indicator.

MO   There are intervals when I don't. Isn't that what everyone does when they are left alone for a few minutes in a room? C'mon, don't make it like it's me. Huh?

DR. OBOLENSKI   Of course, everyone does. But frequency…can… indicate anxiety. So how many times, Mo? Trust me, whatever you say, I've heard it before, everything has happened to some-one, somewhere, *maybe even to me…* So? How many times a day?

   [DR. YOSHIMURA *pays attention to her, also, attracted.*]

MO   I don't count after thirteen.

DR. OBOLENSKI   Do you live alone?

MO   What do you think?

DR. YOSHIMURA   [*To* LIV.] Do you hear voices?

LIV   I don't like to say.

DR. YOSHIMURA   What do they tell you? What do they tell you to do, Liv?

LIV   I don't know. Jump, sort of. Out a window. On a track. It doesn't matter. I won't do it. I have no follow-through.

DR. YOSHIMURA   Do you think you are ready to feel better, Liv? The fact that you came here, on your own, says everything, Liv… That is more than half the battle.

DR. OBOLENSKI   Do you feel ready to feel better, Mo?

   [*He doesn't respond. He puts unlit cigarette in his mouth.*]

DR. OBOLENSKI   No smoking, Mo.

MO   It's not lit. I only suck the filter.

DR. OBOLENSKI   You arrived early, Mo… That's a sign of optimism…

MO No, it's not... I had nowhere to go.

DR. OBOLENSKI I think it is a cry for help.

MO No, it's not.

[THE DOCTORS *confer*.]

DR. YOSHIMURA Listen, this is a good test of the treatment. I would describe both of them as acutely depressed, wouldn't you?

DR. OBOLENSKI I have seen only a little bit more depressed, back in Sitka, Siberia, where I trained.

DR. YOSHIMURA You trained in Sitka? I always wanted to go there. Okay. The Three Pronged Treatment.

MO Don't give me no placebo. I want the real drugs.

LIV Right. No placebo, for me, either.

I don't want to be in a control group.

DR. OBOLENSKI Fine! This is good! The two of you! Look at you! Insisting on treatment!

MO, LIV What is it?

DR. YOSHIMURA It is the three pronged approach. We fight depression from without, within and below. We use drugs, behavior modification and talk therapy in combination...

DR. OBOLENSKI First, we explain: Depression in a social context. That it is global, normal. Every culture has a version of depression. I come from Russia where pessimism is accepted as a philosophy. Our great writers teach us that life is hopeless, love doomed, and we cannot trust even ourselves... We betray our innermost consciences, and commit horrendous crimes for which we are eventually punished. We live lives of dread that are fulfilled in agony!

[*She sounds chipper.*]

So that's normal for us!

DR. YOSHIMURA   And in my country of origin, Japan, a history of oppression and depersonalization has legitimized our rigidity and compulsive conformity.

[*He smiles brightly.*]

We recognize suicide as a logical solution to our problems: It does solve them! And it is honorable! … We have lost touch with the old ways that once sustained us. We are even losing our ethnic physical characteristics as modern Japanese people grow taller and we notice that even our subway cars seem too small for us… We resent living in tiny rooms, on tiny futons. We are not so tiny anymore. Yet, this also makes us disoriented, as we know our respected ancestors would not approve when we drink instant tea.

MO, LIV   What does this have to do with us?

DR. YOSHIMURA   What is your ethnic background?

MO   I think Irish.

DR. OBOLENSKI   Irish. Oh, well, that has its own bleakness, the life of diminished expectations and even those are not met, as the culture conditions individuals to deny themselves pleasure at every slight opportunity. Joy is often confused with sin. There is a morbid preoccupation with The Dead. The only satisfaction is in the grim realization that your suffering on this earth will be finite although you may burn in eternity for whatever moment of happiness you mistakenly knew…

[*She smiles brightly.*]

Right? And alcoholism is a socially accepted way to deal with this state of mind, so you most likely have substance abuse problems on top of your innate cultural and personal despair… Hair of the dog that bit, ya—an tis a very black dog, indeed!

DR. YOSHIMURA [*To* DR. OBOLENSKI.] That was wonderful…

[*To* LIV.] And you, your ethnic background and predisposition toward a cultural form of despair?

LIV Jewish!

DR. YOSHIMURA "Oy Gevalt!" You see I have studied intensely in Brooklyn and the Bronx to understand the psychology of imagined disaster, constant anxiety, compounded by hysteria and a cultural tendency towards overeating and gasid indigestion as a self remedy—"in the kishkas!" for your unrealistically high goals for yourself that predestine you to feeling like a failure…

LIV I didn't think the goals were unrealistic…my parents are both PhDs in physics, and have been happily married and faithful to one another for forty-four years! It's *me!* Give me something!

MO Yeah, just give me the drugs, too.

DR. YOSHIMURA [*To* DR.OBOLENSKI] What do you think…correct the parental imaging?

DR. OBOLENSKI [*To* YOSHIMURA.] It's worth a try.

[YOSHIMURA *grabs* LIV, OBOLENSKI *grabs* MO.]

DR. OBOLENSKI [*To* MO.] I am your Mama. I give you my breast. Ooh…ouchinka, touchinka! Mammala Mammala…Kuchy Koo…

[*She makes kissy noises,* DR.YOSHIMURA *notices.*]

DR. YOSHIMURA [*To* LIV, *also saying this to* DR. OBOLENSKI.]

How's my little Doll? How is Daddy's best girl! I squeeze your cheeks!

[*He makes kissy noises too.*]

[*The patients,* MO *and* LIV, *do not respond.*]

DR. YOSHIMURA   [*To* DR. OBOLENSKI.] Patients unresponsive,
Dr. Obolenski, want to try the much-needed Significant Other?

DR. OBOLENSKI   It is sometimes effective with those who do not have
a Significant Other...

[*She looks for his wedding band.*]

DR. YOSHIMURA, DR. OBOLENSKI   [*To their patients.*] I love you! I
find you attractive!

[MO *and* LIV *do not respond.*]

DR. YOSHIMURA, DR. OBOLENSKI   Okay, prong three: Chemical...
Where's the cart?

[*They push the draped cart toward the patients.*]

LIV   Give me something so I can dream, or just go under...but nothing
that will make me so lethargic I gain weight.

DR. YOSHIMURA   All right, we researched the world over, for a culture
that was not depressive, and we fixed on the Cajun, Creoles from
New Orleans. They had mood swings but by and large a cross
section of Cajun people showed them to be very upbeat—
singing...making love, paddling boats in the bayou, hunting for
crawfish and serving them etouffee... Dancing whenever they get
the chance... We studied their lifestyle and discovered they drank
a particular kind of coffee...

[DR. OBOLENSKI *whips the drape off the cart, and we see a large coffee dispenser,
with tall cups, à la Starbucks, medium, large, larger, and humongous.*]

DR. OBOLENSKI   So what will it be?: A grande latte? Or a vente latte? A cappuccino or frappuccino?

MO   Hey, what is this? Another Starbucks?

DR. OBOLENSKI   You are only partly correct. Starbucks has financed our trial study. We wondered what would happen, if the euphoric effect of lattes and cappuccinos were combined with some basic Serotonin uptake drugs such as those usually employed in Zoloft and Prozac? Cappuccino with a dusting of Zoloft and a dash of cinnamon? They come in Large, Larger, and Humongous. We can give you a cup of coffee as big as you are, in a cup with a drawstring waist and you can dance with it, if you feel good enough!

[*Strains of Cajun music: Zydeco play. The stunned* MO *and* LIV *sip from giant cups.*]

DR. YOSHIMURA   Go ahead, dance… Fay do doh?

[*He smiles, dances a bit, energetically stamps his feet.*]

MO, LIV   I don't feel like it—I don't want you near me.

DR. OBOLENSKI   [*To* MO.] Dance with me. I will squeeze the pain from your body… Hold me tight!

LIV   Sex is no solution. I am always sadder after…

DR. YOSHIMURA   This is not sexual, this compassion hug, to press the pain from you as you drink this exceptional coffee. Please try…

[*She hesitates, then sips. He presses her to him.*]

DR. OBOLENSKI   Mo, come here…this isn't sexual either… I just want to press my Pelvic bones against yours… We can grind out the agony, Mo… While you have a Grande Latte or an Espresso Depresso…

[DR. OBOLENSKI *moves into a passionate dance hold with* MO, *rubbing her cheek against his.* LIV *starts to move a bit, in place, to music.* DR.YOSHIMURA *swings* LIV *toward* MO, *who is being squeezed by* DR. OBOLENSKI.]

DR. OBOLENSKI   [*Husky whisper to* MO.] Let go, Mo, let go of the pain. Oh, I feel it, I feel it entering my body...

    [*She twitches.*]

[MO *swigs another espresso, begins to dance by himself. The two doctors gently guide the couple to one another. The patients,* MO *and* LIV, *still stand, listless, oblivious to the softly playing Louisiana Cajun upbeat sound.*]

    [DR. YOSHIMURA *sighs, puts his arm around* DR. OBOLENSKI.]

DR. YOSHIMURA   How do you feel, Sasha? A bit burned out?

DR. OBOLENSKI   Oh, yes, I absorbed so much pain...my head and breast are throbbing... Oh, Tim, I feel I'm failing them...that it is all hopeless...that nothing can remedy despair...

DR. YOSHIMURA   I love you like a mother, a sister, a friend, a comrade, a fellow scientist and a sex goddess... So what do you say? Sweetheart?

DR. OBOLENSKI   [*Suspicious.*] Did you take something?

DR. YOSHIMURA

    [*Proffering tiny cup to* DR. OBOLENSKI.]

    Medical sample...

    [*Sensual whisper.*]

[MO *and* LIV *begin to dance a bit in place. The music rises.*]

DR. YOSHIMURA, DR. OBOLENSKI   [*Sing Cajun lyric—*]

[*The two doctors sip from one cup, then swirl into the dance. Lights out on the foursome, dancing in manic joy, kissing, embracing, swigging coffee, and fay-do-dohing, Zydeco music blares.*]

[*Blackout.*]

• • •

Her Name Is Kathy

Donna de Matteo

Donna de Matteo

Donna de Matteo is the executive director of the HB Playwrights Foundation and the Playwriting Chair of the HB Studio. She has also taught Contemporary Theatre at the College of New Rochelle.

Her numerous plays have been performed at the Roundabout Theatre; The WPA; Playhouse in the Park; the Cape Playhouse; the John Drew in East Hampton, New York; the McCarter Theatre at Princeton; and the American Film Institute in Los Angeles. In addition, she has had ten plays produced at the Herbert Bergh of Playwrights Foundation, and is a recipient of the Borough of Manhattan's Italian Culture Week Award for performing arts for her play *The Silver Fox*, starring the late Uta Hagen.

Ms. de Matteo's greatest achievements, however, include her two sons, Joseph and Darren; her daughter, Drea; and her successful marriage to her husband, Al.

time

A hot summer night in August. The year is 1957. The time is 10 PM.

· · ·

[BILLY LOGAN, *A good-looking seventeen-year-old young man is seated in the emergency room waiting room of a New York City hospital, Elmhurst General. He is wearing a pair of buckleback chinos; a white T-shirt; a pair of high-top white sneakers and white socks. Splotches of blood covers his pants, T-shirt, socks, and sneakers, and parts of his face and arms. He is shaking like a boy who cannot wake up from a night-mare he is having. He almost starts to cry. To distract himself, he picks up a* Life *magazine. No longer able to hold back the tears, he starts to cry, wiping his eyes and nose on his shirtsleeve.*]

[JACK LANDAU, *a thirtysomething hot-shot criminal defense attorney, enters. He is dressed in a gray suit, a buttondown shirt, and tie. He is carrying a soft brown leather attache case.*]

[*Hearing footsteps,* BILLY, *still sniffling, covers his face with the magazine.*]

ACT I

· · · scene one · · ·

JACK Billy Logan?

> [*Sniffling,* BILLY *picks up his head, and, again, goes to wipe his nose on his shirtsleeve.* JACK *whips out a pressed handkerchief and hands it to him.*]

JACK [*Continuing.*] Here. Use a handkerchief.

BILLY Thanks.

> [BILLY *blows his nose and tries to hand it back.*]

JACK   Keep it.

[*Cracks a joke.*]

I'll put it on my bill. I'm Jack Landau, your attorney. Your father told me to meet you here.

BILLY   Is he coming?

JACK   I advised him against it. The father in him wanted to be here, but the Judge in him knows better.

BILLY   He must be so mad at me.

JACK   He's concerned that you're still in one piece.

BILLY   He told me not to talk to anybody.

JACK   You can talk to me. And whatever you say is strictly confidential.

BILLY   I mean, the whole thing was just an accident…

JACK   Tell me what you told them.

BILLY   Told who?

JACK   The Admitting Office. The Doctor. Anyone that you spoke to.

BILLY   [*Lying.*] I told them the truth. That I lost control of the car and smashed into the side of a building. I was doing about forty when I jammed on the brakes and that's when Kathy practically flew through the windshield. Her whole body just crashed against the dashboard, and all of a sudden, she was bleeding, all over the place.

JACK   Any cops around? Pedestrians? Other moving cars?

BILLY   No.

JACK   …Is that when you called your father?

BILLY [*Lies.*] Yeah.

JACK Where did you call him from?

BILLY Uh, a pay phone…

JACK And how far away from the accident site was the phone?

BILLY I don't remember…I was so confused.

JACK And that's when you told your father you were taking her to Elmhurst General?

BILLY I guess…

JACK And where exactly was the accident site?

BILLY Around 108th Street…

JACK In Corona… A lot of tenements there. Were there any people hanging around outside to cool off?

BILLY …If there were, I didn't see them…

JACK What were the two of you doing in Corona? It's a slum…

BILLY Uh, just cruising around… There's a White Castle there…on Northern Boulevard…

JACK There's a White Castle on Northern Boulevard in Douglaston, too, which is where you happen to live…so why travel….

BILLY …We just wanted to ride around…

JACK …And for no apparent reason, you lose control of the car, crash into a building, where not another soul hears you, and you walk out of the car without a scratch on you, while…what's her name…

BILLY …Kathy… Her name is Kathy…

JACK   …While Kathy was, as you say, bleeding all over the place, you walked to a pay phone, took out a dime, and called your father instead of an ambulance.

BILLY   I was too scared to call an ambulance because I was drunk. …We, uh, drank a bottle of Seagrams.

JACK   …So, she was drunk, too?

BILLY   …Yeah.

JACK   Did anyone here ask you why you didn't call an ambulance?

BILLY   …I think I told them I was only ten minutes away…I don't remember what I told them, I was drunk, confused…

JACK   Billy…you don't sound like you were confused to me. Do you mean to tell me that after drinking a half a bottle of Seagrams, you still had the presence of mind to make a phone call, and then manage to get back into the car and drive ten minutes to this hospital while what's her name was still bleeding?

BILLY   Kathy… Her name is Kathy…

JACK   …How did you even manage to get the car started if the crash was as bad as you said it was?

BILLY   It's a very heavy car… A brand-new 1957 Ford Fairlane 500. My parents gave it to me for graduation. But, if you don't believe me, take a look at the car. It's right outside that door. It's a wreck.

JACK   I saw the car, Billy. That's my problem. You front ended the car into the building. The headlights are gone. The front fender is upended, and the passenger side windshield is shattered. Did her head go through the windshield?

BILLY   …I don't think so.

JACK   Then where the hell did that bucket of blood that is covering every inch of those white vinyl seats come from?

BILLY   I already told you…she went flying against the dashboard! Her head hit the windshield…

JACK   But did any of the glass hit an artery?

BILLY   [*More unnerved.*] I don't remember…!

JACK   Well, you better remember because it looks like that girl was butchered in that car. How did all of that blood get onto the back seats if she was sitting in the passenger seat? The amount of blood in the interior of the car is not commensurate with the exterior damage, which means, something happened in that car before the accident…

BILLY   Nothing happened in the car before the accident!

JACK   There was no goddamn accident, Billy, so let's stop the bullshit! You purposely took that car and crashed it three times into an abandoned tenement building in Corona. When the impact didn't do what you wanted it to do, you got out of the car, took a tire iron, and smashed the passenger seat windshield. There were two witnesses who saw you. Two guys were coming out of the Parkside Restaurant. They thought you were some lunatic so they called the Precinct and gave the Police your plate number. When the Precinct got the alert, the Captain, who thank God is a personal friend of your father, recognized the plate number, because he also happened to be at your graduation party when you got the goddamn car. He called your father right after you called your father with that bullshit story of the alleged accident. Billy, your Dad has had to pull some very serious strings to stop the usual wheels of the system from rolling. Look around you… This is a city hospital. Do you see any cops here yet? Do you see anybody else in this room?

All other ER traffic has been sent to Queens General. Your father is going to owe a lot of people a lot of favors. Now, you have got about five minutes before all hell breaks loose here. So once and for all, tell me the truth. What did you do to that girl?

BILLY   I got her pregnant.

JACK   [*Confused.*] Pregnant?

BILLY   The night of the Senior Prom at Holy Cross.

JACK   What does this have to do with…?

BILLY   That's how it all started…

JACK   By getting her pregnant?

BILLY   She didn't even really want to. She was a virgin. And I told her, "If you love me, you'll let me." I got so excited when she said she would that the minute I got on top of her, I just, well… I never did it before either. I promised her I'd pull out, but it was too late. When it was over, she said I would think she was a slut now. In a million years I never thought she'd let me. We were gonna get married when I finished college. The next day we broke up. We couldn't even look at each other.

JACK   So, when did the girl tell you she was pregnant?

BILLY   Kathy. Her name is Kathy. A week ago.

JACK   How pregnant was she?

BILLY   Two months…

JACK   And what about after the Prom until a week ago? Did you have *any* contact with her?

BILLY   No.

JACK Did she tell anybody else? Her parents?

BILLY No. She was sure her father would throw her out of the house.

JACK And did you tell anyone?

BILLY Who would I tell? My Mom and Dad are so religious, if they were sailors, they'd have the Ten Commandments tattooed on their arms. I was too scared.

JACK So, what did you do after she told you?

BILLY I didn't know what to do. I offered to marry her but she still had another year of high school. What were we going to do with a baby? So, we both agreed to, to…

JACK Get rid of it…

BILLY Yeah… So, I called a Buddy of mine, Joey Antonucci. His brother got his girlfriend pregnant before he got killed in Korea, so I asked him the name of, of, of…

JACK An abortionist.

BILLY But he wouldn't talk to me on the phone. He made me meet him in the Loge Section of the RKO in Flushing. He sat down, offered me some buttered popcorn. I told him I needed the name for a friend. So, he hands me the napkin he wiped the butter off his mouth with, and tells me to slip it into my back pocket.

JACK So, he gave you a name and number…?

BILLY No name. Just a number on a napkin that there was so much butter on, I could hardly make it out.

JACK And so you called the number…

BILLY Yeah.

JACK   And then what?

BILLY   I made an appointment to meet this guy. He told me to bring an old sheet, a box of those things…Kotex; and fifty dollars in cash. And, he said to let her drink a bottle of whiskey before we got there so she wouldn't feel any pain. But, she wasn't used to drinking…by the time we got there, all she kept doing was throwing up.

[*He starts to cry.*]

JACK   Come on, just tell me the rest, Billy.

BILLY   So, we meet this old guy on the second floor landing. The building was pitch black except for this flashlight he was carrying. His hand was shaking so much that the light from the flashlight was bouncing off the walls. I saw a rat this big running across the hall. I was ready to leave right then and there, but Kathy said no. The old guy takes what's left of the bottle of Seagrams and drinks it himself. Tells me to stay in the hall, …not to worry…he's done this a million times, he says… Then he brought Kathy into this apartment and slammed the door.

JACK   So, you were never in the room while the crime was being committed?

BILLY   No, but I could hear her screaming through the door. Jesus Christ, I didn't know what to do. I was so scared.

JACK   …And then what happened?

BILLY   She stopped screaming. I waited for five minutes and walked in. And that old drunken bastard was gone. He must've ran out of the fire escape window and Kathy, was on the floor, on the sheet, covered with blood. I never saw so much blood. I wanted to call an ambulance, but she said we'd both get arrested. That's when I got the idea to make it look like a car accident.

JACK   My God... And then what?

BILLY   She couldn't walk cause she had these really bad cramps, so, I wrapped her in the sheet, carried her down the stairs and put her on the back seat of my car.

JACK   And that's when you crashed your car into the tenement? Was the girl still conscious at that time?

BILLY   Jesus Christ, for the last Goddamned time, her name *is* Kathy.

JACK   Wake up, Billy. Her name *was* Kathy. The girl is dead. She was dead when the attendants got her out of your car. Her parents are on their way here and they are going to want to know, "How did this happen?"

BILLY   [*Buries his head in his hands.*] I am sorry. I am so sorry...

JACK   [*Puts an arm around Billy's shoulder to console him.*] "How the hell did this happen?"

[*Lights fade to black.*]

• • •